One Leg Out

A Tragicomic Memoir

A LITTLE BOOK ABOUT THE MENOPAUSE

WITHOUT THE FLUFFY BITS!

'The past is your lesson, the present is your gift, the future is your motivation.' - **Unknown**

'A successful woman is one who can build a firm foundation with bricks others have thrown at her.' - **paraphrase of quote by David Brinkley**

For Steve,

for putting up with me and my crankiness.

GATOR HOUSE

Published by Gator House, an imprint of
Gator House Publishing LLC
North Charleston, South Carolina
www.GatorHousePublishing.com

Copyright © 2018 Carla Day
Cover Design & Chapter Sketches © 2018 Blake Marsee
Editing provided by Gari Strawn

Gator House Publishing is a United States based publishing company.

PUBLISHER'S NOTE

First Edition

ISBN 978-0-9997335-9-2

Diary Entries

One Leg Out

CARLA DAY

One Leg Out

Dear Diary,

Festivals and Hot Flashes

Today is a rainy day in Wales. It's quite soothing listening to the rain pitter-patter on the windows while I sip sweet coffee and think about what to tell you today. My garden is dying off, all the colour is diluting, and the garden furniture needs a lick of paint. I love in between seasons when things aren't definite, and summer and autumn get into a dance of hot and cold and the trees begin to moult. I'm moulting too, it's menopausal, I'm shedding my lovely thick hair.

Work is going well but is poorly paid. It's such a shame because the job is so rewarding, even if I do work with oddly behaved but very entertaining staff. The good people make the job great, it's a bit like attending clown school for adults, lots of silliness, bickering and sometimes, fun. I have had hints that the manager might have me earmarked for her job as she is nearing retirement and seems to be showing me the ropes. The words haven't been spoken, however, the gestures suggest it's a possibility.

Do I want it? I think I do, then I change my mind because of how chaotic the place is. The relevant QFC qualification in health and social care is being pursued, so it's definitely an option and there is room for growth there too. I hope she stays well enough to teach me everything, as she indicated she would like to, she's not a particularly healthy woman, and I do worry, I worry about everything. Managers so wonderfully encouraging and friendly are few and far between. Let's see. I'm not a planner and have been known to be easily distracted and thrown off course. If my writing should ever take off and make those elusive millions, then, screw the job. I'm just being honest, Diary, we all want to do something we truly enjoy that also pays well, you can't have it all, right?

My first book has been accepted for publication and I'm delighted. I don't know if it will make the shelves, I'll do all I can to make that happen, though. I hope my story will reach a few hearts. Either way I'm proud of my cathartic novel. It took guts to write, and I've never had guts before. I'm now wondering, will it be good enough? Is it well-written? Is it a steaming pile of self-obsessed shite? Only my readers will know the answers, I suppose.

My son is off to a music festival, his first at only sixteen, he's camping out with mates, God, will my heart hold out? — Hello, sleepless nights. After the recent tragic events in Manchester, my heart is in my mouth and I will have the urge to pull him back into the house and tell him he can't go, of course, I won't but I really, really, want to. I let my exotic birdie fly. His exam results are due, and I desperately hope he gets the results he has worked towards. I have a little knot in my stomach for him. He's worked so hard, a little squirrel that lived in his bedroom, studying day and night.

I'm proud. I know he will be hard on himself should he not get the grades he is aiming for. I've told him repeatedly; his best is good enough. This has kept me awake a couple of nights of late. It's silly because I know he'll smash it. The brown envelope will be here on Wednesday and I'll be so excited I might wee a little — it's menopause related, Diary.

My seven-year relationship is getting better, improving with age. We are getting close again after battling with personal demons. I think we are realising we're forever and there's no need to fret over silly things. We are stable and solid — apart from when I get all menopausal, and then it's not so stable, more like funhouse floor at the fair. It took time for us both to understand how to be grown up about relationships and maintain trust and belief, but I think we're there now, apart from when we are not.

The house, however, is driving me nuts. We have just enough money to start to make small changes to it. I call the house "Mr. Void." It's a cheerless shell that needs a personality. I like a nice home, not fancy but at least finished and the tattiness of it seriously gives me a headache, especially when neighbouring houses are finished, we look like the poor neighbours. Pass the wine.

I miss my family, being far away can be tough and I feel the weight of guilt. I mostly miss my mum and want to speak to her but every time I do, I feel as If I'm speaking with someone else because of how her voice changed after becoming ill. It just makes me cry. Everything makes me cry, even adverts. I have been avoiding talking to her. I should call because it's not fair to her. I say, 'I love you mum' every single day. I don't know if I say it to the heavens, or if I hope the whisper will reach her bedside, or if I say it because I feel guilty. Mmm, I need to go sit and hold her hand and tell her about my life. She must feel abandoned or does she still have issues with time, does she know it's been almost a year? Fancy going and having a stroke, you silly moo. I'm going through the change, and I desperately need to talk to you.

I'm fat. Diary, for the first time in my life I have a middle bit, a squishy overhang that drives me nuts. I grabbed a handful of it the other day and thought, *Oh-My-God, I'm officially middle aged.* I don't feel it, but I certainly look it. It made me laugh too, this bit of me that will not shift no matter how many miles I walk or how many mountains and hills I climb — and that's not a metaphor. I need to work blasted hard if I really want to lose it. It's a stubborn ring that's made me buy bigger clothes and worse, I own no less than ten pairs of Bridget Jones pants. I look like I've swallowed one of those giant-prawn Iceland party rings whole — not that I would ever buy them, Diary. I like home-cooked food, but I have little enthusiasm at the minute for looking amazing or eating like a rabbit. I'm giving myself a break, looking okay is fine. If I need to do a book launch or something, then I'll do a quick, drastic diet and run like Speedy Gonzales until the spongy stuff melts away — I know it's not that easy.

The menopause isn't too bad now, thank God! I honestly thought I was being punished for something I had done in a previous life. It felt like I was dying from the inside. I guess you are really, in some respects. Medication was the key and a clear mind — although, in my case, perhaps it never really is completely clear. The changes to me and my face aren't that bad, not really. Hopefully, I'll feel like facing people soon with my new middle-aged look.

I've avoided those I love for a long time. It's funny, I look in the mirror some days and wonder where the fuck I went — I apologise for my profanities in advance, but they are, at present, the largest part of my vocabulary and "the F word" seems to be a particular tonic. Other days, I welcome my new face and smile at it like you do when you are unsure of someone. I'm getting to know it, and it's not that bad, not really. Who am I kidding ... it's a stranger's face that is more wavy at the edges and it's going to take time to fully appreciate but she's growing on me, the old bird.

I need to go and see people soon. I've kind of mended my heart, not completely, but I keep sticking plasters over it, and it's in one piece. I hope to remove those plasters soon and let it beat freely. I'm so used to missing the people that died, the hurts subsiding, leaving just the happy memories and a pinch of pain. I've locked away most of the bad ones. They can fuck off because they cause havoc with my intermittent, but debilitating, depression. Again, thank you, Menopause, for increasing my anxiety attacks and spurring on my foul language and zapping away my confidence.

Today is a good day and I feel happy even though money is tighter than ever. The last week of the month is always a struggle. My boy needs to get a job to have money in his pocket. I try and push him without stressing how much I need him to earn a little money of his own while he studies for his A levels. Is that wrong? He is nearly seventeen. My wages only just stretch for the two of us. I was waitressing and worked two jobs by the age of fourteen. My lovely man helps wherever he can, but he shouldn't have to. He's my son. Mmm, that's a whole chapter of its own.

Anyway, I'm signing off for today, I'm not going to write you every day, just when I need to talk because my mates are far away, I guess you'll have to do.

Until next time...

Dear Diary,

Gold and Glittery

I know I said I wouldn't be visiting every day, but it seems I have stuff to get off my chest. I've just come back from a long dog walk on the beach. The sun was high in the sky and made the water on the estuary gold and glittery. A warm breeze rustled my hair and made me sigh out my stresses. Work was challenging today, one of the senior — by senior, I mean older — members of staff was griping and bitching about absolute nonsense for no other reason than, I believe, she's losing the plot and I fear she may just be a bit on the senile side, I know this from experience, I forget stuff daily.

One Leg Out

The woman is a whole decade or so older than me and can be a smidgen bitter about life. She does a lot of teenager-ish sulking which makes me chuckle and at the same time want to throw something at her or bludgeon her with a frying pan — again, menopausal related anger. She has a vinegary attitude toward life that irritates me.

I was very proud of myself, Diary and managed to keep schtum while she talked to me as if I were five, mainly because I was taught to respect my elders. Really, I wanted to vomit words of venom at the bloody witch and melt her into the ground with my well-practiced death stare, but I was very grown up and bit my tongue. She is, I'm convinced, on the tail end of the menopause and possibly doo-lally because of it, so I can forgive her a little bitch-and-moan, God only knows I've had enough of them myself lately but fortunately, for now, I'm able to keep them out of work.

I keep telling myself, *WE are all human and must allow for one another's gripes*. Sometimes, though, my reasoning just doesn't wash. I'm just not accustomed to bitchiness and don't see the point. What is to be gained from it? I must be a hippy, all love and peace, eh? Talking of hippies, my boy's first trip to a festival is looming over me in a cloud of tangible fear. I've brought him some Buddha beads and a bandana which he actually liked — bonus.

Tomorrow, I'll be waving him off and will not be able to hug him because his mates will be there and that's "so not cool." Five days, OMG, five long days, I won't sleep until he's back and if it rains I'll be in the car off to Reading to rescue him. I know I'm being ridiculous, he's practically a man. But he's my exotic little birdie and my baby. Ha, all mums are the same, right? He was stressing earlier about packing and getting stuff ready and was getting real moody. I managed to calm him with a bribe, the shameful promise of a Mac's burger after my dog walk, even though I wanted to stick one on his chin. Kids can be grumpy, ungrateful gits. It's strange, I love him to the moon and back, but boy, can he ruffle my feathers when he's being a shitty teenager. I'll be tearful the minute he's on the bus, ha.

'Mum, can I take a suitcase?'

'No, son, you're going to a festival, that's not cool.' I did a smug smirk because — for reasons beyond my reckoning — the menopause makes you do funny stuff like that.

'What would you know about cool?' he asks.

'I know plenty, you need to stick with the rucksack, that's what they are for.'

'But my friend is taking a suitcase because you're only allowed one item of luggage on the bus.' I check with the bus company and find this is not the case.

'No, son, this will have to do, it's going to be muddy and you are in a very small tent, you have to use the rucksack.'

'But why?'

'For God's sake, son, just trust me.' I tell him he can have a Mac's to throw him off course and stop him asking stupid questions.

My man's away and the house is stupidly spotless. I keep walking around admiring the neatness and that clean smell that lingers after a thorough scrub. It always happens when he is away. As much as I miss him, the house stays tidy and shiny and things are put in the places they are supposed to live. Within seconds of him being home the house will be so messy I'll spin around chasing my tail, putting shit away, and sighing my fringe out of my eyes while the mountain of shit multiplies over chairbacks and banisters. Shoes will be left in the middle of the floor and dirty washing will spill out of the laundry bag and I'll drink a nice *large* glass of sufficiently room-temp-warmed red wine, so I don't nag the living daylights out of him or explode my furious brain matter across the walls — this is all menopausal, of course. I've developed an uncontrollable temper.

I have to focus on the telly, so I don't see the mess ... God, men can be untidy creatures. Yes, I know — stereotyping isn't cool but damn it, it's true. Anyway, I can't wait to see him because I hate it when he's away and the wine is warming as we speak. Out with the son — sad face — in with my man — smile. Don't worry, Diary, I'm officially a bit mad. My initials are CJD — also the initials for Creutzfeldt-Jakob disease — AKA mad cow disease. It's true, how ironic.

I have two days of training coming up which I am dreading because it seriously bores me to death. I'm not kidding, I could actually topple off my chair from boredom and have a nana-nap under the table. The company will be great, but we will be expected to act serious and answer ridiculously stupid questions that bear no real relevance to our jobs. Usually, the questions are all, roughly speaking, the same, just worded differently to stretch out the day and brainwash us into uniformity. At least we will get free tea, coffee and biscuits — oh, best not, moment on the lips! Who am I kidding? Of course, I'll snaffle them away while assuring everyone this is the last day of feasting before my diet starts. I'll even convince myself that a couple of custard creams won't hurt because tomorrow I'll be eating courgette spaghetti and sipping green tea.

Well, that's it for today, talking about work's bitch-fest made it seem pretty trivial, thanks, Diary. Oh, I almost forgot, my dogs got her period and I brought her a tiny nappy. She looked a bit mortified, but it's stopped her spotting all over the floor. She doesn't seem overly impressed with it and won't look me in the eye, ha. Spoke too soon, she's ripped it off. The mop bucket is now my only ally.

Exam results in on Wednesday – eek!

Dear Diary,

Nail-biting Times

Well, the exam results came in. It was on the first day of my training with work and the farce of trying to email the results to my boy who was at Reading festival was a bloody nightmare and got me into a bit of a sweaty panic. I wanted him to see the results before my enthusiastic family started to bombard him with congratulations messages. I told them first in my excitement but had promised him he would be the first to know. My reception was terrible, and he couldn't open the attachment. I digress, he did brilliantly — no — fantastically, and the training therefore was bearable because my son is an actual genius, and

Carla Day

I beamed with pride all day. I even became tearful when explaining to colleagues that my son was simply brilliant. It seems several other mothers' sons were geniuses too.

It's weird, my boy's success is far more important than my own. His self-worth is a huge deal because I didn't have any, I suppose. The relief was immense. Not that I didn't believe he would achieve great results but because I know how high his expectations are for himself. What might have been a success in my eyes might have disappointed him. I needn't have worried though because I heard him smile down the phone when I eventually managed to speak to him.

The excitement lingered for a few days, then, I turned my thoughts back to my fatty bits and a trip to the Lake District that was playing on my mind. I was going to be climbing Scafell Pike, the highest peak in England with my man. Great, you might say, but of course, I'm going with well-seasoned, super-fit hikers. I am experienced but fat and chubby hikers are frowned upon, even if it is never said. It is the same crowd I hiked with in Bulgaria, where I huffed and puffed my way up several mountains, always traipsing at the back. For the entire trip, I promised myself I would be fitter for the next time.

Here it is and I'm still a bit of a heifer and mad with myself for not starting that well-intended diet that I have been on the verge of for more than a year after the menopause made me two whole stone heavier than my normal eleven-stone weight. Okay, maybe three.

One Leg Out

I've started waking in the night, terrified I'm going to embarrass myself by glowing scarlet, blowing out of my arse, sweating profusely and lagging, slowing them all down, like I did in Bulgaria. The shame was unbearable. The damn trip is giving me nightmares. I made a last-ditch attempt to abandon the carbs and gobble up mountains of salad. All of course, far too late, you can't lose a stone in three days no matter how many steps you run up and down in your pajamas when no one else is in the house.

I worried for nothing. I managed to do it relatively easily. I'd worked myself into such frenzy and imagined the climb to be way beyond my ability. I had imagined it to be a monstrous hill that would engulf me, when in reality it was far easier than Mount Botev in Bulgaria. The weather was cooler, and I even managed to enjoy it and wasn't too out of breath to manage a conversation as we climbed.

Still, I want to be fitter. I want to look like the young French woman that comes with us, the ex-ballerina, a successful businesswoman, who does the splits on mountain tops and looks the part, even if she knows it. The sight of her makes you say, 'For fuck's sake,' under your breath while forcing out a believable smile, good on her — skinny cow. The thing is she's also a very lovely skinny cow.

Oh, Diary, why am I never happy being me? I do blame the menopause though. I blame it for my unusual mental state, my persistent anger, my ability to be uncharacteristically forthright and my constant questioning of myself. I blame it for my ugly use of language. I could seriously turn the air blue.

As I pace along my menopausal journey like a caged tiger, the anger is my most disturbing attribute. My poor fella isn't quite sure what I'm going to come out with next. I'm sure some of my shocking statements make him gasp in disbelief or horror. I'll give you an example:

While he was preparing a meal and asking me, 'Do you fancy some pudding?' I bit his head off. 'Why would you ask me that? You know I'm trying not to eat puddings, why would you show me a fucking trifle — you are a selfish shit!' I'm salivating and give in to the offer of trifle and cream some minutes later, after which I attack him again, for being a selfish knob.

I've even used the "C" word in an argument which is at the top of my list for disgusting words and makes me scrunch up my nose.

'That word, really?' he says, raising a patronising eyebrow. I don't understand why I can't just simply say, 'No, thanks.' And smile.

I have become blasphemous at the slightest opportunity. I have a strange, beguiling need to tear strips off my man just for being there. I can't control it either. Something about him makes me angry. Everything about him makes me irritable. I love him, I adore him, but I sometimes want him to suffer like I am suffering. I know that's wrong. I know if I don't control this inner demon, I will push him away, but the scary thing is, at the precise moment when my venomous vocabulary is unleashed, I don't really care, it's afterwards when the damage is done, I regret my runaway potty mouth, and the brief return of sanity makes me feel like an utter shitbag.

Then I cry myself to sleep embarrassed by it all while pretending to still have the hump, so he doesn't see me cry. Go figure.

There is a whole league of tortured women out there, previously thought of as insane, batty as a fruitcake, nuts, off-the-wall, lunatics, or just plain absurd and dotty, who might actually be menopausal. Thank God we are not living in the Victorian era where my menopausal insanity might have been misdiagnosed as hysteria. I might have been carted off to the asylum for wayward girls, rape being the only cure for my idle lady parts. Thank God we have moved on from those times but still, we haven't managed to still the mind during this cruel metamorphosis from youthful to middle-aged. The chemical and hormonal imbalance when a woman is going through the menopause makes thinking itself confusing.

Sometimes, it's like trying to figure out a math problem while submerged under water, wearing goggles and mittens, and then not having a pen to write the answer with anyway. It's impossible, firstly, to figure out the answer, secondly if you did figure it out there is nowhere to document it and thirdly, what the actual fuck is happening to my brain? Forgetfulness, Diary, is something else. I actually wrote a shopping list to take to the supermarket because I didn't trust my brain to remember the items I needed for a well-practised recipe. But I shouldn't have worried because I didn't even remember to take the list or my purse. That was on a good day.

I remember a comedy incident that happened once in a supermarket that made me cry with laughter and is something I can actually imagine doing myself, at times. I was following a middle-aged woman who was pushing a trolley around the aisles because I liked her red shoes. A young twenty-ish woman who not looking where she was going accidentally nudged the woman in the back of the knees causing them to buckle, and the middle-aged woman dropped a carton of milk onto the floor.

The older woman went into a complete psychotic meltdown and physically attacked the poor "pretty" girl who apologised repeatedly while being battered about the head with a fake Louis Vuitton handbag. The older woman seemed to relish the opportunity to hit someone and plainly enjoyed the episode. She calmly walked off afterwards, leaving a gaggle of shoppers speechless. The young woman was in total shock. Maybe it was the menopause. Maybe she didn't have a man at home to take it out on? My God, I need to get this anger thing sorted, maybe my HRT needs changing again. Or, maybe I should take it out on a pretty girl too, or I could ask my doctor to check my hormone levels. There's a battle in itself. Doctors only seem to want to do that test once and when it's confirmed you are indeed menopausal, you are expected to get on with it and are bullied into taking HRT. There's no mention of all the alternatives out there. I'm seriously sick of the medical profession when it comes to help. They seem to know very little.

Anyhow, in four weeks, Diary, there is another trip to the Cotswolds for yet another hiking weekend, guess who's going? Yes, that's right, the ex-ballerina who speaks multiple languages, poses mid-split on the top of a mountain for a photo, earns shed loads of money and travels the world because she can. Yes, her. I am going to try and lose the spongy middle bit at least and be a stone lighter. I'm also off to my sisters for Christmas and there is no way I am going if I am still fat, for two reasons.

One, I have upset my sister's boyfriend by writing that I don't like him in my memoir, then managing to get a publishing deal for said memoir. Mmm, that meeting might be a tad tricky, and if I'm going to have to grovel a bit, I might have to look amazing while doing it. Two, they have never seen me fat, and I won't be able to handle the jibes, even if they are innocent enough and meant to be funny. I don't trust my new-fangled forthrightness. I might shout at them or attack them with a shoe or some other inanimate object. So, if that isn't motivation enough, I don't know what is.

I'm checking out now. I'll be back soon.

Dear Diary,

Holding My Tongue

Today has been a relatively peaceful day, a day of reflection. On my calming morning walk along the estuary, I decided that I am going to do my best to control my outbursts and tantrums. While watching cluster of dead jellyfish bob about on the surface, I spotted a live one speeding through the water, desperate to catch the far-away tide and be washed back out to sea, to safety. I felt a strange amount of empathy for the little thing chugging through the calm millpond, wanting to get back to where it belongs, and it triggered something in me. A longing to feel how I used to — good. I realised that without a huge amount of effort, I wouldn't be able to feel good about myself. I decided there and then to start to change the way I speak to my man and to bite my tongue and to get to the doctors ASAP to try and figure out why I'm being a complete bitch, why I can't lose weight, and why I have little willpower to do anything other than eat, write, and walk.

I had an epiphany. Only I can change the things that are making me miserable. Several minutes after, a man came through on his bike at break-neck speed and gave me a filthy look because my dog wouldn't budge from the middle of the path. I was so proud of myself, Diary, because the word 'WANKER' was just waiting to spill out of my mouth.

Instead, I just said, 'It's a dog walk too, not just for bikers, you know!'

For one horrible second, I thought he was going to stop. I'm glad he didn't because I haven't got enough self-control yet and don't entirely trust myself not to attack him with the dog lead, but he kept on peddling and I kept on walking and it felt good to take back a little control.

So, today was a good day. My head is clear. I'm going to call the surgery first thing to try and get an appointment, new pills, and maybe some light counselling. Let's see. I'm not having tea tonight, I've eaten enough calories for today, go me!

Dear Diary,

Smells of Home

It's raining heavily, and I don't want to go out, the sky is dark and misshapen inky clouds have blossomed, blocking out the softer, paler ones behind and everything on the ground is soaked. The trees smell delicious and the aroma of the earth reminds me of being small and walking with my dad in autumn on soggy leaves.

Diary, you would be so proud of me. I took myself off to the supermarket three days ago and in a wave of excitement I filled my basket with all the bizarre ingredients for weight loss. I'm going to do Slimming World but without actually going. Isn't it nuts? I don't want to be weighed until I've already dropped a few pounds, I'm too vain and just not in the mood for the self-loathing that smacks you around the face when you realise you are at your heaviest. I don't need scales to tell me that, thank you very much.

My goal is to get my favourite size fourteen jeans over my hips. Just over my hips would be marvellous as they currently won't budge past my wobbly thighs, even a trusty coat hanger won't do the trick. I want to have a ceremony when this happens and burn my current size eighteens in the garden, I might even build a bonfire. In fact, I'm going to build one. That's a way off yet but I'm in the right frame of mind and I'm walking daily, the poor dog's knackered. By Christmas, I will be back to the old me, or at least as near as possible because I'm not contemplating plastic surgery. The new face will have to do and maybe some new makeup.

As we speak a chicken casserole is bubbling away in the slow cooker. The fridge is brimming with Tupperware boxes containing my nutritious breakfasts and lunches. Healthy snacks have been prepared so I don't fall of the dietary wagon. I am not going to drink alcohol at all. Not until Christmas. Now, I might be reading the wrong signs, but my son said to me today after three days on it, 'You look different, Mum, younger.' My first reaction was to ask him, 'Did I look old yesterday?' What was he going to say, poor lad. 'No, Mum.' It was a random compliment, and he didn't even want anything. He doesn't usually comment on my appearance because he knows better. This act of kindness spurred me on and made me want to go for a run and keep my diet momentum up.

This time I haven't made a big deal about my diet, or in fact, told anybody because if I make a big deal of it and have a small lapse, I'll never live it down. Especially after *many* previous failed attempts when I've caved as my son asks, 'Fancy some ice cream?' Not just any ice cream but Ben & Jerry's, I mean, who could resist? I would jump in the car and be motoring towards the Co-op within seconds for two gorgeous, glistening tubs. Eating the ice cream was *heavenly* but immediately after, I was disappointed with myself and wishing I hadn't eaten the whole tub which I would eat with a teaspoon, so it lasted longer. I'm determined to stick to it this time. I have actual goals. I want to feel smug in my nice expensive Rab bubble coat and be able to zip it up, instead of pretending I keep it open because of my menopausal flashes. My damned hips.

Work is the same, recently we had a week away and the core staff stayed for the entire week while some stayed behind. It was entertaining to say the least. I shouldn't comment on colleagues but there is so much comedy material, it's unreal. An all-woman-staff can be bitchy at the best of times, and when I say bitchy I mean they could open an over-forties circus for sarcasm and pettiness. I can see them dressed in stripy stockings and orange wigs, throwing wet sponges at one another and mock crying.

Throw in the menopause, age related forgetfulness and differences of opinion and you have the makings of a bloody clown war. I've never heard such rampant tittle-tattle in all my life. I'm sure my eyes were actually spinning by the end of the week. At one point, each of the women — who individually seem very nice — repeated the same sentence about something that needed to be done, one after the other. Then all argued about it, even though they agreed in principle. It made my head hurt.

I like to sit back and watch the entertainment unfold while pretending to watch TV in the communal kitchen. I was washing pots that didn't need washing. I daydreamed about taking them out one by one with a ping-pong bat. Is that terrible? Fuck it, I don't care. I'm surprised I've not ambushed them with my newfound poisonous tongue. Thankfully, work is the one area I manage to keep my thoughts tied in a knot and in my head.

Just.

Anyway, Diary, as I said, it's entertainment and not much makes me laugh these days.

My boy is working, yay! He has a part time job in a restaurant while he studies for his A levels. I almost fell to the floor when he said he would be washing pots because he will not touch the pots at home, no matter how much I try to bribe him, even Ben & Jerry's won't do it. I always believed that he was afraid of germs or found old food disgusting or some other OCD trait had made him afraid of touching dirt. No, it turns out it's just laziness. My boy is lazy around the house. I need to train him up. Anyway, Diary, thanks for listening, I'll keep you posted.

Dear Diary,

Panicking Over Nothing

It's my treasured day off and I've decided to make the most of
it. After a lie in until midday, I've come to my favourite spot by
the estuary for a walk with my dog. I'm on a path that runs
parallel to the beach. It's a strange old day, it's mild and the
estuary is carrying in a gentle, warm breeze in from the open sea.
The air is still, and it doesn't feel like October at all. I've parked
myself on my weather-beaten log with a take away coffee —
skinny, of course — and a notebook and pen. I do most of my
thinking when I'm at this place and don't want the thoughts to
drift off into the ether without documenting them to report to

you, you know how forgetful I am. Dog walkers are ambling by, some not noticing I am here because they are all staring out to sea, lost in their own worlds.

I had a bit of a weird night last night. Recently, my sleep pattern has been erratic as in I haven't really been sleeping at all. I decided to buy some herbal tablets that promise a decent night's kip. I'm tired and feeling ropey enough in the day to not function well. I've never been good on zero hour's sleep. The evening started fine, after a nice relaxing bath and a bit of mindless TV, I swallowed down the little white pill — which smelled a little bit like feet and dung.

Not long after, I was drifting into sleep, but something was niggling at me. I hadn't considered that my need to be in total control would cause a problem. Inside my head, a battle had already begun. My partner came to bed shortly after and I had a sudden need to be awake. It became a desperate need to stay awake and I couldn't breathe because my head was fuzzy, and I was having a monstrous panic attack. I ran to the window and threw it wide open. I took in big gulps of cold air and prayed they would help me stay awake so eventually I would fall asleep naturally.

My partner tried to stroke my head to calm me down, but the warmth of his hand felt claustrophobic, and I just needed something to concentrate on. He began to ask me questions to take my mind of feeling out of control. It didn't work, so he switched on the TV to give me something to focus on. So, with windows blowing in cold air and flapping the curtains in my face, the TV blaring out and my partner stroking my arm. I eventually fell asleep, exhausted. I am not sure what I am afraid of. Why was I fighting the very thing the pills were designed to do? I don't understand myself sometimes. I clawed at wakefulness when I had been desperate to sleep.

I have been prone to panic attacks throughout my life. Even when I'm in what I consider to be a good place, they still pop up and take me under. I've never fully understood why but I do know they are terrifying, even if they are just tricks of the mind. But that was last night, and I mustn't dwell in case I bring on more of the blasted things.

Diary, I'm still on my diet plan and going great guns. I am so determined to be healthy that I have managed to ignore the coffee cake that has appeared in the cupboard. I even managed to not shout at my partner for bringing it into the house. This is a monumental step because it means I have conquered self-control. I can safely say after six days on plan that I have self-control, how wonderful is that?

I'm doing long shifts at work and enjoying time with the girlies, I'm even able to say no to the amazing cakes that are produced by our very own star baker. I live in an area where I don't know many people, which is fine, although I'm not a recluse, I've become comfortable with my own company but it's nice to know a few like-minded people. We are organizing a few nights out, which gives me hope that I may settle here after all.

Carla Day

I had a meltdown a few days ago which made me really mad with myself. My son happened to be in the car having a lift to college. It was after a particularly bad night's sleep, where I dreamt about starving puppies that I couldn't reach, as the corridor kept on growing as I ran and ran — I'm not even going to try and analyse that. I was predictably grumpy, and I directed my confusion and anger at my son because his phone bill was high. I lectured him all the way to college about responsibility nodding my head and pointing my finger and I couldn't stop the words as they spilled out and he got out of the car shaking his head. I'm sure he thinks his old mum is a nutter. He's not far wrong, either. Anyhow, I rushed to the shop, once I'd realised what a tit I was being and brought him two toffee apples and left them on the kitchen counter with an apology note, a pizza, and a chocolate milkshake. I always feel bad after being an idiot so why can't I just not be one? Am I a bit loopy? Again, I blame the menopause.

This takes me back, Diary, to my second encounter with *the change*. The first was up a mountain which I'll tell you about another time. I was in a supermarket and I began to feel warm but not in a way I have ever felt before. It was a feeling that crept up from my upper-middle back to my neck and then my face. Before I could really decide what was going on, I was sweating profusely. Luckily, I was in the freezer section, I milled around the frozen aisle pretending to look at the frozen peas, with my head literally inside. I pulled out a bag of broad beans for tea once the feeling subsided, I do love broad beans. It happened again in the car, and I thought I was coming down with something.

A week later was my first ever appointment with the doctor about my illness. I was convinced it was CANCER. The symptoms were all there: night sweats, hot flashes, soaked sheets, morning tremors, and a general unwell feverish feeling that I had never experienced before. The poor doctor I saw was not long qualified and had me, the menopausal wreck, to contend with. I'll never forget the look on his face. His brown eyes glistened with the smugness that youth brings, and he couldn't have been much older than my son, surely? It took one question for me for physically crumple into a sobbing mess, 'How can I help you?' I saw a look of panic flash across his face as he frantically flicked the pages of some sort of manual — yes, Diary, a fucking manual. For some random reason, I poured out my feelings about the grief after losing both grandparents. I left his office with grief counselling sessions booked, nothing else I had been worried about was discussed.

A week later I was back and relieved to be greeted by a woman doctor who I guessed was middle-aged. She asked me a number of questions without making eye contact which made me nervous. She then said it could be the perimenopause. I laughed. 'I'm only forty-three,' I confirmed, hoping that would be an end to that nonsense. Then, she went on to explain that although it was highly unlikely, all the things I had described seemed to point to the beginnings of the menopause. That told me, then. She

Carla Day

asked when my last period was, and I couldn't remember.

Diary, it was the beginning of a journey that is memorable for all the wrong reasons. It's only now, four years later and still in the midst of it, I'm able to see it with humour. Oddly enough, looking back it was pretty funny and still is, but at times it can feel like I've fallen into a pit of snakes, and I'm constantly trying to avoid attacks. I think it takes a period of adjustment to understand that it needs serious management and continual assessment to keep the bastard under check. It also takes a tough cookie to deal with all the unfair stuff that happens to you and a brilliant sense of humour.

Ha, a dog walker has just stopped by with his big yellow dog, we exchanged notes on having bitches and talked about how mild the weather is and he went on his merry way. I love how friendly dog walkers are. In the beginning, Diary, when I said I had the menopause under control, it seems I spoke too soon. Sleepless nights and foggy heads are back, the hair thinning is more noticeable. I have to blow dry my hair a different way to disguise it and irrational thoughts are creeping back in. Oh, and did I mention my eyesight is failing? My optometrist disagrees. He said, 'It's age-related,' as he breathed his uncomfortably close curry breath all over me. I have an unusual amount of floaters, and I seem to be looking through a veil when peering at a white wall or an empty sky. It's all due to age. If I've heard it once, I swear. Anyway, the edges of my vision sometimes seems as though it's darkening. Oh, the joys. I'll get another opinion because he didn't listen to me, and I'm sure after consulting Doctor Google that I am going blind.

Diary, I'm not sure if I'm being silly but my neighbour, who is a year older and has no signs of the menopause yet, is running marathons all over the place, she looks younger than me and it annoys me. I keep seeing pictures of her on Facebook, holding up her shiny medals to the camera and smiling with superbly white teeth. Her eyes seem to be boring into mine, saying, "See, if I can do it." Part of me thinks, *just you wait until you go through it*. Isn't that awfully petty? She's sweet but I can't help feeling jealous. Is that normal? It seems unjust that I started this process earlier than others. I feel robbed of an extra few years of a tight jaw-line and thick, glossy hair. Gotta go now, Diary, apparently, I'm needed in the kitchen.

Dear Diary.

Animals and Differences

Well, my good intention has fallen somewhat short. I find myself continuing to snap at my lovely partner who scratches his head in bewilderment and wonders what the hell is going on. If anybody spoke to me the way I do to him sometimes, I would have to kill them. Kidding apart, Diary, I'm concerned that I am unable to control the awful things I say. Even when I know as they tumble out in inexplicably coarse sentences that they are plain wrong. It's not me. I swear there is someone in this head of mine that is sniggering and willing me to do it.

I am trying not to let little things niggle at me, like when my dog is shut in the utility room when my partner is alone downstairs watching TV. The poor thing is alone in the house during the day and loves company when we are home. When I see her sad little eyes peering at me through the dark, I want to take a screwdriver to his skull. I ask, 'Why is she in here?' 'I didn't know she was,' he will say, and it makes me mad because of course he knows, and he isn't caring in that way although I know he would never harm her. Am I in the wrong? She is a smelly little girl, after all who scratches her ears and rubs her bum along the floor and can be distracting when you are watching telly, but still. He won't pick her up and give her a cuddle. If he does lift her up, he holds her at arm's length and pats her on the head as if she might have fleas.

My grandma had always told me to be wary of men that didn't like animals. It's not that he doesn't like them, but he is selective about the type of animal he likes. For example, if the breed is good and the animal isn't the runt of the litter, he will find it more agreeable. Whereas if the animal is a bit scruffy looking and has one ear — the type I'm drawn to — he will sort of turn his nose up. In my eyes, that's not an animal lover, is it? I'm rambling but I have always been an animal lover and will cuddle anything that looks unloved, no matter how smelly or scruffy.

I know that we are not all the same and it doesn't make him a bad person, for I know he is not, but why can't he love animals more authentically? Another thing that is really getting on my nerves is the fact that his obsession with rugby is not just a healthy passion as I once believed but it literally takes over the best part of the winter and all our plans revolve around when matches are on. Maybe I'm being petty, I love that he has a passion, I just don't want it to be all the time and so distracting from our joint hobbies. I suppose it's down to the fact apart from walking and writing, I don't know enough people here yet to have a full social life. I depend on him, to a degree, to entertain me in my free time. See what I did there, Diary? I talked myself around. I often discuss problems with myself and resolve them too. Aren't I clever? I'm at work and have a free period where I can entertain myself and I've forgotten my book, so I'm talking to you.

This morning a member of staff, who is a genuinely lovely person but for some reason can't seem to grasp the massively important routine that we have put in place for the autistic people we support, is making my day really fucking frustrating. How can I tell her without being a patronising prick that she is cocking the entire day up with her tiny mistakes? Gosh, I'm good at swearing — I just can't. This is what makes me mad, she's a relative stranger who I've known for a short period of time and I don't want to hurt her feelings. Yet, a man who shows me love and affection, no matter how horrible I am, I am a complete moron to. You know that old cliché — you can be more frank with those you are closest to. I don't think that's fair, why should they put up with the shit when all they want to do is care for you and see you happy? Life's weird, Diary, and I've concluded that maybe I am too.

I should take this dear woman aside and tell her she's really, really not so great at the job, but I really, really like her anyway. No, that won't do. I'll ask someone else to do it. No. I'll ignore it and put up with it because it's kinder, and she's such a lovely person. There's nothing wrong with being kind, and I'm sure she'll catch on.

I've done something stupid, Diary. I have accidentally dyed my son's *brand-new* white hoodie he brought with his very first wages pink. I was holding the evidence in my hands in our utility room, examining it if as it were a dead animal and holding it to the light to see if I could get away with it when my son came breezing through to use the downstairs loo. I panicked and chucked it in the bin and then stood by the bin, not allowing my son to throw in the empty loo roll on his way back through.

'What's got into you?' he asked.

I looked at him with such apologetic eyes. He just shook his head and took the loo roll with him. Do I: a) fess up, b) buy him a new one and then fess up, or, c) pretend I haven't seen the top since he brought it? No, I can't do that. Can I? I'll think about it.

Dear Diary.

Water Mills and Cockle-Shells

Okay, I may have been a little hasty in my decision to become suburban mistress of supreme sophistication. I miss the countryside. I should have listened to my inner-self years ago and become a farm-hand, instead of gallivanting all over the place in the name of love and adventure. Maybe I should have stuck to cows, pigs, and chickens.

Once upon a time, not so long ago, for a whole wonderful year I lived in a rural, nomadic place at a rundown watermill.

One Leg Out

Not only was the place a lot drafty and full of uneven floors and wonky ceilings but it was by a river and the gentle noise of it trickling day and night was soothing and peaceful. That place came at just the right time. It was in between moving back in with my partner and after a stint of caring for my mum which completely messed with my head.

I felt calm there and most importantly, I was away from the world's eyes. I liked being self-sufficient, don't get me wrong, Diary, I didn't grow or kill stuff, or anything like that — even though I had my pick of chickens that shat on my decking most days, they so deserved the cooking pot — but I cooked casseroles and walked in the hills and forests. I did a bit of crafting and a lot of thinking. Pheasants would screech as they ran wild, and the neighbours were so eclectic and wonderful, I felt safe, even though we were out in the sticks.

Here, however, in suburbia where there are a multitude of shops, streams of people and busy crowds, I feel lonely because they are not my people and the older you are, the more difficult it is to make new, genuine friends. There are a number of reasons for that, confidence at present is at an all-time low, and I just don't go anywhere I'm likely to meet folk because by nature I like lonely places. I've always been comfortable with my own company and can easily entertain myself. I've been known to shuffle off out of the way of society for periods of time when life gets too much.

Diary, I suppose what I'm trying to say is that I'm getting the urge to do it again — run. It's definitely because of the menopause because I couldn't really imagine living without my partner no matter how much we tussle around one another's emotions. But it's so difficult to live with myself, being ratty all the time. I often think it would be better to battle this thing alone, with no fear of residual fallout. Go to war with it, see who wins.

I don't want to have to explain my fluctuating moods and symptoms. I just want my suffering partner to naturally understand but then, when you find it hard to understand yourself, of course he can't. Even my son, and, Diary, he is more than my world, as you know, but I could run away from him too. Obviously, not because I don't love him, Diary, but because I want to spare him my desperation, anger, and weird mood patterns.

My son asked me not long ago, 'Mum, why are you so angry?' This was after I'd exploded about something unimportant. My answer was, 'Because, son, life can be fucking unfair.' And you know what, Diary? He didn't bat an eyelid. Now that can't be normal, he stomped upstairs, sighing like teenagers do, with purpose. It's not right for a child to listen to his mum cursing, I see him wince when words fall out of the air and paint it. I never swore in front of him when he was small, I could hold my tongue then, I had some integrity and control, where has it gone?

I guess it's an ordinary thing, to want to run for the hills when you believe you are the problem. Sticking around is harder, but it's the grown-up thing to do. If I can't grow up when I'm at menopausal age, then I'm truly screwed.

You know, dearest Diary, I had another blooper moment a few days ago, brain fog returned to have its fun with me while I sat at traffic lights. I was trying to compile a shopping list in my head while the lights were on red. Not an unusual thing for me to do but a strange heavy-headedness lodged itself in my brain and made me squint to try and concentrate. This is how it went:

'I need medicated shampoo. I wonder if I can use human shampoo on the dog. I heard you can use eye drops. Bless her, she's getting old and smelly, do all old things stink a bit fusty? Maybe the walks are getting too hard for her? And with her legs being so short, she must be sick of having a muddy belly all the time. I suppose you can use human stuff on dogs, you must be able to buy all kinds of lotions these days which reminds me, I need a good cream for the cellulite on my thighs and perhaps some tanning lotion to disguise it if a good massage doesn't shift the orange peel. Lube, I have to get some, my partner is going cross-eyed from the lack of sex. Sex, urgh. Right, concentrate, I need tomato puree and minced beef for spaghetti-bolognaise, I wonder why they call it bolognaise, is it a place in Italy, it must be. Shame we're not going to Lake Garda now, I was really looking forward to it. Kitchen roll, the dog had a little accident in the kitchen and I had to use a tea towel and chuck it out after. Air freshener, do not forget air freshener.'

Diary, by the time the lights were on green, I forgot the shop, drove straight home, picked up the dog, and took her for a lovely walk along the beach. Which is fine but when I returned to the house there was no shampoo to wash the dog and nothing for tea.

Damn you, Menopause!

One Leg Out

Dear Diary,

Funny, Warm Day

This morning was decidedly strange. I left the house at stupid o'clock for an early shift and the sky had turned sepia, as if I were in some noir style movie. The breeze was unusually warm, and the birds were silent. There was an apocalyptic feel about the day, and it only got stranger. As I pulled into the drive at work, I felt a very calm sensation wash through me as if I had taken some kind of drug. I can't really explain it apart from it was transient and was over as soon as I walked through the door.

Carla Day

I am calmer in general and I'm weaning myself of the HRT. I've read that if I do this cold turkey I might end up in the looney bin, so I'm doing it gradually, but I've already noticed a marked difference to my buoyant bust, it's slowly deflating, thank the Lord, I don't think there is a size I could go up to. I got spooked because I'd heard on some daytime chat show that if you take it for too long there is an increased risk of blood clots and as a natural worrier, I have convinced myself if I don't come off it, I'm going to have a stroke or a heart attack or get thrombosis the minute I step on a plane — not that I'm planning to go anywhere, Diary, but you never know.

I've managed a civilised conversation with my partner with no bickering, and we even had a hug in the kitchen. Things are looking up. I didn't have the urge to clout him with the kettle. Maybe the HRT was making me cranky? I haven't eaten cake in two weeks, get me.

One Leg Out

Dear Diary,

Marigolds and Wet Weather

It's windy in Wales today, trees are bending, and branches are snapping, thanks to storm Brian. It's wetter than an otter's pocket and far too miserable to go out walking, and I'm in desperate need of a walk. You know how my mental health suffers. The sky is gloomy, a monotonous stream of grey, no depth, just endless pale mist. Brrr.

I'm going to spice things up a bit in the bedroom. Things have dried up because of my eternal lack of libido. When I say things, I mean my vagina — why do I cringe and bite my lip when I say

Carla Day

that word? It's drier than Stephen Fry's sense of humour, drier than the Sahara, you get the picture. I have tried topical creams and local estrogen pessaries and none of them really do anything to moisten up the area apart from a bit of Vaseline. I think I need to be in the right headspace for self-moisturising.

I recently learned from a daytime chat show that if you don't have regular sex during the menopause, it — my vagina, cringe — could literally shrink inside and scar tissue could form and Oh-My-God, that is just another shocking fact about the menopause. Basically, use it or lose it was the general consensus of the show. So, I need to get my act together, buy a vibrator — which might just give me a panic attack — and start to seduce my partner on a regular basis, to Hell with the pain, I'll get used to it. I'm pretty sure he won't mind.

I was a complete nymphomaniac — okay, slight exaggeration — when we met. He must feel like the unluckiest bloke in the world. From sexy, horny woman with voluptuous curves and an insatiable appetite to, 'Don't touch me or I'll seriously hurt you.' Poor man. Anyhow, I'm going to buy some sexy undies, classy not tarty, I don't do tarty unless I'm a bit drunk. The nearest I came to being adventurous was a nurse's outfit which was so tight, it gave me lumps in strange places. I felt ridiculous, until my man showed his appreciation in an unprecedented, very manly way. He likes me to dress up, who knew?

Anyhow, I don't feel comfortable in sex-shop-brought shiny stuff and definitely no gimp masks or patent-leather, but a good

One Leg Out

pair of M&S nicely cut, silk and lace panties, and balcony bra, maybe a pair thigh-high boots, do make me feel sexy. Good underwear equals confidence. It's funny, I like to be bathed and smell gorgeous, fragrant and to have my make-up and hair done, then, I feel ready to be loved.

My man would be totally happy to bend me over the kitchen sink once a day. He does like the effort, of course, but I think men in general like sex when and wherever. I think even my pink marigolds would count as dressing up. I believe men are just happy to be having it.

Emotional attachment lies more with the ladies, that's what I reckon, Diary. I must ask, do all men think with their willies, or is that a generalization too far? I do recognise the cavernous differences when it comes to sexual appetite between men and woman. I know their hunger can be desperately primal.

I honestly believe that if a man is getting regular sex and eating good food those simplicities are enough to keep a smile on their faces and their heads turned towards their partner, rather than straying. Even this lingering thought hasn't made me have sex more frequently. At times I've even thought, 'Please, go have it somewhere else, just don't ask me.' Not that I really meant it, I'd be utterly devastated, but that's how horrible the menopause can be. You honestly risk stuff that's important. I love sex with my man. I love the intimacy and the closeness and the other sensual feelings too. It's just the getting started with me. I need jump leads.

Carla Day

How come, in the beginning, I had my knickers off before we reached the landing and now the thought of sex makes me sigh? Why does it change? I do think that if the menopause hadn't reared its ugly head, we would still be at it like knives — where does that expression come from? It sounds painful rather than sexy. The same as 'at it like rabbits,' that just make me think of myxomatosis.

Anyway, Diary, a trip to M&S is in order. I've been off my HRT for a while, and although I'm a bit more agitated, as in I want to hit someone at least once a day. I seem to be sleeping better. I'm not so knackered during the day. Hoorah, a small milestone. Maybe that hasn't helped either? I've been a tired, grumpy mess of late.

Perhaps, I can successfully seduce my man if I'm not so bloody drained all the time. I'm going to have to time it just right. I'll make my move after my son is in bed, or when he's at work, not when rugby's on and before I fall asleep. Mmm, it might be tricky to get the timing right, after all. I can just see it. My man will come to bed just as I've nodded off in my nice silky undergarments and he will be frisky, and I will have dribble running from the corner of my mouth, it might even have dried into a crust. I will feel massively unsexy and the urge will have died, and I will want to sleep so very badly. He will try and cuddle up to me and definitely fondle a boob and I will snap because Mr. Helmet will be knocking on my spine.

I simply can't do it when I'm tired, but he won't come to bed early because telly has become his ritual. Catch-up TV means he can watch every single rugby match in the universe. Mmm … He has to make an effort too. I'll let you know how it goes. I might

try and seduce him while rugby's on, that might be his ultimate fantasy. I'll even wear a rugby shirt, let's see. Ha. Made up today, Diary, I had my birthday tan-leather biker-boots today.

Thanks for listening, Diary.

Dear Diary,

More Rain in Wales

Well, Diary, it seems I have gathered enough stuff in my head and I need to empty it out to you, so I might be here a while. Can you believe, I've just had a few days off work and it absolutely hammered it down. I'm talking monsoon-style rain and gusts that knocked the car about.

Today, low and behold, just as I threw back the curtains *before work*, expecting a grey sky, the sun is streaming in through the window in ribbons of gold. Sod's law.

I've missed vitally important walking days and that is not good for my mental health — I need the walks so my mind doesn't

One Leg Out

clutter, luckily, I have you. I mean what is a girl supposed to do when stuck at home for days on end? The natural course of actions is to grab a duvet and fill your face with treats while watching chick flicks but as I'm on a diet, I can't. Diary, it's been hellish trying to keep my hands off the sweet stuff. Every time I opened the fridge door a trifle with its frilly colourful layers has stared me in the face, goading me to eat it. Not to mention the full-fat yoghurts and the bloody luxury tiramisu. Grrr. Even though I've visited the fridge frequently, if only to look at these delicious items with fraudulent contempt, I managed not to eat any of it, not one sliver. It was the longest four days of my life. I've paced the house, ran up and down the stairs repeating my mantra: 'You will not be a fat bastard by Christmas.' After fifteen laps, I opened the fridge door just to stick two fingers up to the sodding treats. It felt good too. Luckily, no one was home to see me battling with my temptations, I might have looked a bit of a silly billy. self-control remains in my court.

I've had my thinking cap on today as I drove around and around for work. Christmas is just around the corner, as you know I'm fasting for the visit to my sisters, but it also means I'm going to be out of pocket. I'm going to spend a serious chunk of my wages on my son and his driving lessons, theory and practical test as that's what he wants for his Christmas and his birthday, which is two-days before. But as it isn't a tangible gift, and he will most probably be grumpy if Santa doesn't bring something substantial to open, I will also buy him other bits which won't be cheap

Carla Day

because he doesn't like anything cheap. I suppose, Diary, that's just parenting — giving, giving, giving. I do love spoiling him though.

Another thing that has been eating away at my mind lately is the lack of communication with my friends, it seems when you are away, it is a case of out of sight, out of mind. Unless I call or text or message them on Facebook, I wonder if they would call at all? It's a funny business because stubbornness makes me think, 'Sod them.' I'm not calling if they don't which is silly. If I miss my mates I should call them and let them know I'm thinking about them but then, what if they don't want me to, and what if they have new friends because I'm not there — head-fuck. What if they don't really like me because when you miss someone you keep in touch, right? I tend to overthink stuff, as you know. It's really stupid though because when I do go to my hometown and see people, it's like I never left, so I surmise I'm being a dick but my mind, as you know has a will of its own. Anyway, rant over, I love sorting my problems out and having a good old debate with myself, is that normal? Let's hope so.

My next issue lately has been the amount of money I'm spending on diet food. It costs a small fortune. Things like: chia seeds, avocados, quark, wholemeal, a ton of salad and veg, nice lean meats. To do the diet successfully, you need to make sure the food cave — aka the fridge—is brimming with healthy nutritious snacks so you don't pick at the bad stuff. I'm telling you it's costing significantly more than usual, and my purse is squeaking with fear when I open it. I physically shrink a little when I get to the till at Tesco because I know it's going to make my eyes big when the cashier tells me how much my rabbit fodder is going to cost. 'But at least I'll be thin,' I repeat all the way to the car, ignoring passers-by as they look at me like I'm a bit nuts. Do I care, Diary? No is the answer, I've stopped caring. Ah, that's better.

Tonight, I'm working until late but at least it's not with one of the demented staff. Although comical, they can be brutishly tiring. Tonight's company is a pleasure. Also, my partner's away, so I get my big queen-sized bed all to myself, and I can starfish my way to sleep in fart-less, snore-less, wild-flower, fragranced bed – YIPEEEEE! More than a night and I'll be pining.

Carla Day

Dear Diary.

Grey

I had intended to only visit you when there was something important I needed to say, but this endless rain has made me turn to you, again. I'm going stir crazy inside my unfinished house. The sky hasn't altered in three days, the sea of pale-grey is suppressing. There's a constant drizzle that ruins any efforts you have put into straightening your hair and soaks you to the bone within minutes. It's not even the type of rain you can comfortably walk in. It's totally miserable and I feel like I'm suffocating.

Getting out and about is my catalyst for happiness. There is only so much cleaning you can do when trapped inside and I'm not a huge fan of it anyway. I end up making a puppet show out of dusters and cleaning cloths to amuse myself. Give me a pair of hiking boots and a hill to climb any day. I do the bare minimum when it comes to cleaning, and I would happily pay a cleaner to do the mundane stuff. Life is to be lived, what is the point of dusting your way through boredom? My partner doesn't agree with the paying part. He would rather leave it messy and do a weekly tidy together but when he says together he means, he will faff about while I do the lion's share because I'm quicker and more thorough and he knows it. The thing is, although I don't like cleaning, I can't stand mess. You see my quandary, Diary. It irritates the shit out of me to see stuff everywhere. So, I have to do it but without complaining because my lot are totally happy to live in a chaotic home and would tell me not to bother if it bugs me so much. I've kind of backed myself into a corner.

I have been watching a daytime women's gossip show because I'm off work today and I saw an odd clip of Kim Cattrall, the sexy cougar from Sex in the City. She was chatting to Piers Morgan on his ridiculous but enjoyable tell-all show and was talking about her non-involvement with the other women from the fabulous show (I think I had a bit of a girl crush on her once.) She was saying that they really don't have much in common because of the age gap and the fact that she doesn't have children and they all do.

She smacked of menopausal-ness, I know that's not a word, but

I do like it. I can spot a menopausal woman from twenty paces. It's a kind of uptight, pinched, and exhausted look that gives it away and the impromptu frankness that prevails when you get to the point of just saying it as it is. Menopause is great for that, it lets you say what's on your mind. I believe this is a temporary filter removal, a mask that you wear while menopausal that can get you into all kinds of trouble. It's something you can shed, once the angry undercurrent subsides.

I'll give you an example: A woman at my work, who is in her sixties told me it's only now after over a decade of going through the menopause she is beginning to feel like her old self again. *Oh, fuck, really?* was my initial thought to that, only another eight years of insanity left to go, then? I have read about this a lot too. It's as if we changelings are temporarily possessed — if you can call a decade temporary? While our brains try to catch up and figure out what to do, how to act. I can say with conviction I'm not the same person I was before the menopause because I know I feel differently about everything. Emotionally, I'm rawer yet more defensive too. I've lost my easy-going personality and I am very quick to be rattled and jump to my defence or anybody else's, if I feel they are being wrongly done by. It's very strange and an obvious hormone imbalance but it does make you feel like you are going a bit mad, or madder than usual.

The other obvious changes are the physical aspects, the agerelated sagging and other humiliating traits that I won't go into because the list is endless and growing — nasal hair growing quicker than my actual hair being my least favourite. My breasts are humongous, I mean they are painful and full and God knows what with? I've had the same bra size my entire life and now I don't know what to do with these super-buoyant monstrosities. Suddenly I have to look for different style tops than I'm used to because my shape is more apple when it used to be a definite voluptuous and very lovely pair. I loved my pair and my medium-sized, manageable boobs. Diary, I could cry at the loss of them.

Anyhow, the spottable differences in women who are going through it have become more and more obvious to me. There is a fundamental look, a look of bitterness, masked with, 'It's okay, I'm fine.' Most menopausal women are not fine, they are only just coping and more often than not with depression, husbands that don't get it, a stressful, full-time job and daughters going through pre-menstrual cramps and turmoil's while looking young, shiny and beautiful, and sons hiding in their rooms going through constant-masturbation-syndrome.

I'm not criticising, how could your family possibly know what you're going through, when no one bloody talks about it?

Why is this topic not being discussed? The entire planet is crammed with women and every woman will go through this at some stage during their lives. Should they not be pre-warned of the undeniable changes to everything? Relationships will be tested, even the strongest. Sanity will be pushed to the outer edges of reason and your body becomes a battlefield, not to mention painful nipples — what's that all about? Shouldn't every woman know and be armed with as much information as possible to help them go through this demonic period in life?

Yes, I believe they should. Yes, Diary, I really believe they should. Because, Diary, if I would have known just how tough the menopause really was, I might not have found it all so bloody shocking.

Thought for today: *Share with all females you meet who are past the age of forty your honest, crappy, experience.*

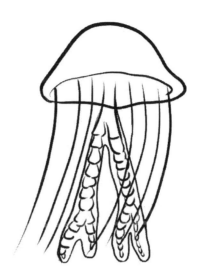

Dear Diary,

Together with Seamed Condoms

I've been dying to talk to you! I've been so busy and today I promised myself, after my gorgeous walk in the gloopy autumnal sunshine, that I would get my thoughts out. My partner and I walked along the North Gower Peninsula basked in gold as the wind swept through our hair. It was a beautiful, clear day and, although I started the day exhausted and groggy from not enough sleep, I managed to wake up and feel fresh and wide awake. We needed this time together, it's rugby season and I was getting a bit pouty, feeling left out.

Carla Day

As we ambled along the shore line, I spotted what I thought to be a pale pink condom, lolling about in the shore sand, fully inflated with a seam down one side. My eternally-curious dog went over to have a sniff and I kicked it with my hiking boot, not entirely convinced it was actually a condom. My dog picked it up and started to run, that's when I noticed stringy, electricblue, frilly tentacles coming out of the end. 'Put it down, now!' we both bellowed because it was a deadly Portuguese Man-OWar jellyfish. Luckily, she left it and scuttled off with her tail between her legs. We continued to walk through lots of inflated condoms. It was a strange and funny sight that made us giggle and tell silly immature jokes. The colours on some of the fresher jellies were vibrant and amazing. They are such fascinating creatures. It was sad to see so many of them washed up. I managed to step on a couple without seeing and they popped like balloons. I was scared to touch my boots when removing them in case their jellyfish juice might poison me.

I wondered how long jellyfish could survive out of the water, the answer is: The man-of-war is *not* a jellyfish. They're a siphonophore, a single animal made of a colonial of organisms working together, and they don't last long out of the water but their stinging tentacles — which can be as long as five red buses — can still be fatal, especially for dogs and small children, lucky escape for my wee dog then, phew.

We stopped for a coffee and walnut cake on the way home. Yes, the diet is *off* for today, it's a treat day. Don't tut, Diary, please. Then, we stopped for a fruity cider and a pint of ale in a posh pub where they served salty cashews instead of peanuts, all very lush.

My exhaustion is due to my sleep pattern, which is, once again, erratic. I'm back to one leg out of the quilt. I say the quilt, but I actually sleep with a light-weight fleece blanket covering me or half of me depending on my internal thermostat. My other half has the super-togged duck-down quilt folded over him. He sometimes flicks it on to me in the night and then I toss and turn and get so overheated, I feel like crying.

We have a discussion every night before bed. My partner will ask me, 'Is the window open?' I will say, 'No.' It is open, of course, but I need it open because if not I fear I will die of heat exhaustion. He knows it's open because he can hear the traffic outside and will close it while I sulk and call him an insensitive prat. I wait until he is asleep and open it again. I toss and turn umpteen times and take the fleece off, and then I get chilly, so cover myself with said fleece, again, this cycle continues all night while I stick my leg in and out like I'm doing the hokey fucking cokey.

I would genuinely love to know how many times I actually turn during the night and does this count as exercise? I don't think I sleep more than a couple of hours, so I feel grumpy for a while when I first wake up. If I remember, I close the window. Is it because I'm off my HRT? I'm not having many hot flashes, but the weather is generally getting cooler. Also, Diary, I don't sweat

Carla Day

during the night, so at least the bed stays dry, small miracles, eh? My moods are not too bad, apart from when I'm tired, which is all the time. Ha. Anyway, my fella's cooking me a nice Sunday roast while I write to you, so I can relax a bit now.

Let's hope I sleep tonight, I won't but as I'm off work until Wednesday, I can have a lie-in tomorrow, I can sleep during the day, no problem, why is that?

Something has bothered me, it's not a new thing, but it really got to me today. My man and I disagree on as much as we do agree on. We were discussing perhaps one day when we are old and thinking of retiring that we might become wardens for a caravan site. It appeals to both of us. We love fresh air and travelling and camping, etc. The conversation was going well. We talked about how we could rent out the house while we moved around the country mowing lawns and maintain lush sites.

Our current neighbour is a grumpy old sod and my partner said that he might get bad neighbours which made us do an evil snicker. It was all very amusing until my fella said this, 'He might even get Pakis next door.' I had to do a double take, this bothered me for a myriad of reasons. It was a ridiculous, sweeping statement and I know he meant Asian, Pakistani, Indian, or other races of a similar colour. He absentmindedly huddled them all into that one pathetic title. It made my blood boil, Diary. I explained that what he just said was not only politically incorrect, it was offensive, racist, ignorant, and he sounded like an uneducated fool. I asked, 'And what would be so bad about having a Pakistani family next door?' He tried to worm his way out by saying that it was only the same as someone calling him a Taff. This infuriated me on a new level. I said that they would be absolutely right because he was WELSH!

Pakistanis come from Pakistani, not India or other neighbouring countries. I had to stop talking because that stuff really grips my shit, and my brain was about to explode. We are so far apart when it comes to these fundamental issues about life.

I think he realised he said something spectacularly dumb, but he still defended it, which made me want to cry with frustration. Oh, Diary, I do find this so disappointing. I'm very liberal minded and carefree and love-thy-neighbour. I've always thought that so long as someone's happy with their lot, be they gay, straight, of differing ethnicities, gender neutral, whatever, that's okay, life's all about being happy, surely? I would love neighbours of any nationality and would endeavour to be a good neighbour, we can all learn from difference. Why can't the world hold hands and get on in spiritual, harmonious unity. Joking, sadly. I know that just isn't possible. My partner isn't of that ilk, and he can be quite brutal when it comes to opinions on race, religion, gender, and politics. It's good to have an opinion, of course, but when it's a bigoted, single-minded one, it makes me seriously uncomfortable. Should I avoid talking about it all together, or be a grown-up and agree to disagree? What happens when we are out socialising? These issues are common topics, do we argue it out in public? Can a relationship survive with such cavernous gaps in opinion? I suppose it must because I love him.

Rant over.

Dear Diary,

Bitchy Times Ten

On today's walk on the beach, I was accompanied with brain fog and heavy legs. The sleepless nights are catching up and the crankiness has ramped up a gear. After an hour and a half, plodding alongside the sliver of estuary that was left, as the tide was out, I still felt heavy headed. It seems someone has replaced my brain with cotton wool while I slept, or not, as it happens. I took myself off to the weather-beaten log where I'd scribbled notes for my memoir and sat a while, hoping the magic might return and the fresh air and Mac's coffee might clear the cobwebs. It didn't, my mind seemed to jump from thought to thought. It went something like this — after seeing a young woman jog by, her golden ponytail swishing, with her loyal but somewhat knackered-looking yellow dog trotting behind with its foamy tongue lolling out.

That woman's hair is amazing, so thick and glossy, I bet she's not menopausal, bitch, she looks too fresh. Fresh cream, I wonder if I'm allowed it on the leftover rhubarb pie in the fridge, of course I'm not. Ooh, I need to clean the fridge, it's been a while and it's a bit stinky. My dog is whiffy too. Perhaps I should bath her when I get home, I need to pick up more dog shampoo, I've run out. Shampoo, everyone's using my fucking shampoo, I'm the only one who buys expensive shampoo. When they buy it, it's the cheap one-pound stuff from Home Bargains. I should hide my shampoo. Where can I hide it? Roots, I need to dye my grey old-lady roots, they're becoming obvious, I fucking hate getting old. I can think that word because no one can hear it, fuck, fuck, fuck. (Laugh to myself.) An old man walks by, no dog but a walking stick and very sad eyes. I wonder if his wife's dead, or his dog. I wonder if he eats okay, maybe he's ill? He looks a bit yellow, perhaps he's dying. Why am I being maudlin? Maybe he's enjoying the sunshine just like me. I need to go home via Pets at Home. Where's the dog? (She's wandered off and is sniffing a lump of sea vomit.) 'Come on, girl, let's go.'

I watch the man disappear from view before I get up to go. It takes all my effort to move today. I forget to go to Pets at Home.

One Leg Out

I forget everything. Menopause has a lot to answer for. Forgetfulness is something even I have to laugh at. I just go with it. I say stuff like: 'You know, what's her name, big tits, sings country and western.' Diary, if I can remember all that why can't I summon up her name? Thingy magigy, what's it called and thingy bob, are all common phrases in my everyday life. I remember stuff when I no longer need the information. It's a pain when I'm trying to get involved in a conversation. I have to plan ahead so I don't sound like a nincompoop. Even then, names escape me. It's just menopause and it's not consistent. It's just a nuisance sometimes. 'Where are my keys, who's moved them now?' I ask when they are right in front of me. Hey ho.

My boy, oh my, did he get it in the neck the other night, I'm still unsure if I was to blame or not? It ended in a text war which made me feel like complete kaky-poop. It was the weekend, I fancied a couple of drinks, not wine just cider and a TV night because everyone except me was going out. I played taxi, dropping him off with fruity ciders packed into his rucksack and believed my boy was going to a local Halloween party and would be able to walk home. So, I proceeded to drink a couple of ciders and enjoy the peace, and I got into bed in my pajamas and caught up on stuff I'd missed on the telly. I received a text at midnight asking could I pick him up from a place that wasn't local, he'd moved venues. I said no, I'd been drinking, he would have to stay over or walk. He reminded me that I'd said I would be able to pick him up if it wasn't after two a.m. Of course, I had forgotten saying

Carla Day

this and immediately became defensive. I told him that it was selfish to expect me to lose my licence and irresponsible. I asked him, 'Why couldn't I have a night to enjoy for myself?' and told him he could walk, it wasn't far and he needed the exercise, so there! And my text rant went on and on. His sarcastic replies implied he was seriously pissed off. You see, Diary, even though I knew I was in the wrong because I did say I would pick him up, I verbally attacked him for being selfish. What's wrong with me lately? HRT, that's what. I've been off the good stuff long enough for the withdrawal symptoms to kick in. Foggy head, sleepless nights, on the plus side my ginormous breasts, thankfully, have deflated, a little. The forgetfulness, the crankiness, the low energy, the sarcasm, it's all part of not being on the drug that replaces estrogen and progesterone.

What a head-fuck. I don't want to be on HRT for years because the health risks are high. The doctors tell me that if I don't take it, I'm at a high risk of osteoporosis or heart disease but if I do, I'm at even greater risk of having a stroke, breast cancer, and possibly fatal blood clots. It's a confusing minefield. I don't know what to do for the best. I want to tough it out, ride the storm and come out the other side fixed. I have no idea how long that will be. I don't think I can feel this way forever, I might hurt someone, or myself. It's a horrible way to live. I'm knackered, exhausted, and moody. I have no sex drive, no tolerance, to anything, even my own voice. Why, God? Was premenstrual tension and childbirth not enough? If I don't get this sorted I'm going to have a serious brain-fart. Argh, I do have good days too, although they are becoming increasingly rare. Should I just go with it? Perhaps when I adjust, I will feel better. Please let that be soon, Diary. Thanks for listening.

You know, Diary, I said the sweats had all but stopped. Evidently, as I sit here mopping my face with a towel, I was mistaken. It's back. Why can't it just go away? I desperately want to stay off HRT. But will I be able to cope? Are my symptoms going to come back and engulf me? I find doctors next to useless. So, going to them is not an option, they will try and scaremonger me into believing my bones are going to crumble to dust if I don't fill my body with this fake hormone.

Hmm. My gut says stick it out, it can't last forever, can it?

Dear Diary,

Cravings

There was once a time when I would have killed for a night out, dancing, innocent flirting, and good old let-your-hair-down drink. Not that I'm dead and don't get the occasional urge to go out and party, Diary, but the things I do crave most have changed quite a bit.

Now, I crave the outdoors and great views, I literally feel the pull of it. I want to breathe fresh air so deep into my lungs they might to explode. I crave a good book and a cup of tea. I crave a night at a friend's putting the world to rights over a glass of wine.

One Leg Out

I crave amazing vistas. I crave antiques fairs and crafty days. I crave black and white movies and chocolate. I crave new places and quiet.

The social difference between the things that I once craved and those I do now is simply because of age and that's natural. I enjoy different things now: new music, TV programmes, red wine, radio stations for older audiences. The things I like, that are the same, such as going out to watch foreign movies at the cinema, drinking coffee in antiquated book shops and walking in the rain, I appreciate them more as life's so short.

I like to focus on stuff I would have once merely glanced at because I love the small detail. I love how I have the ability to laugh at youth and their fickle ways without underestimating their importance to the future of the world. I love to sit on a viewing bench and drink in every sight without ever getting bored because I understand how precious every second we have is. I like that I can laugh at myself, Diary, even when I'm really mad which is often.

Now, Diary, there are times still when I let trivial annoyances get to me as you know, but I do try my hardest to let them pass quickly because any kind of harbouring negative stuff is such a waste of time.

Another thing I've been thinking about a lot recently is where men stand for the duration of the menopausal-y journey.

Us ladies expect our men to be kind, compassionate, understanding, loyal, and most importantly, quiet when we are going through the change. I genuinely feel sorry for them because they are underprepared and uninformed, and the reality of what happens must surprise the shit out of them. They must suffer terribly too and feel insecure, unloved, and frustrated. Think about it, Diary, the woman they grew to know and love suddenly becomes someone entirely new and not in a good way.

Everything about their woman is different, at least in my case: physical appearance, emotional instability, weight gain, cursing, and anger outbursts. I'm sure there are times after one of our many petty arguments, that my partner would have celebrated my departure should I have actually gone when I threatened to which was at least once a fortnight.

He has put up with sarcasm, flippancy, sexual rejection, demands, hurtful remarks, and madness. I'm honestly not surprised some men don't stick around. If the situation was reversed, I'm almost certain I would have left long ago.

In our defence though, Diary, learning to reach out to women about the menopause, I have asked a lot of things. The scariest of my finds is that there are believed to be approximately thirty-six symptoms of the menopause, and most women suffer around ten of them while on their unique journey. That's some serious shit to deal with while trying to get on with busy lives.

Dear Diary,

Happy Birthday to Me

Despite a sweaty, uncomfortable night's sleep — yes, the sweats have returned at night too — it's my birthday and I'm in a happy place. My partner despite having spoilt me already buying the boots I wanted most in the world also surprised me with perfume, a card, and a cup of tea in bed. Aw, today I could squeeze him to death and not because he's annoyed me by leaving his socks next to the laundry basket to wind me up — he won't find it quite so funny when I sneak them under his pillow.

The minute he left for work I got myself buttery toast, with extra lashings of rhubarb and ginger jam. Yes, Diary, it dripped through my fingers, and I didn't give a damn. I licked it off and sipped on my coffee. Yes, it had sugar in. Well, it is my birthday. My plans for today are to get all my happy thoughts on the page to you, then go for lunch with my son and a walk on the beach. Boy, I'm predictable but I just love it.

When I first woke this morning, it was to the ping of my phone as birthday messages flooded through. It's a weird feeling, the blatant lack of birthday cards no longer matters because you get wishes from people you haven't seen in years, I love that. Still, on my birthday I feel special, even if there is nothing particularly eventful going on. It's an inner self-smugness, a today-is-my-day feeling. I always try and book my birthday off work, so I can love myself and spend it doing exactly what I want. That might be sitting in bed munching on toast — to hell with the crumbs — and watching morning telly and drinking copious amounts of coffee and sniffing my new perfumes. I got three. I know my boys got me a present, Diary, and this time it's from his own wages. That melts my heart. I want him to wake up, I might turn the telly up, very exciting. Even if it's a really pants present, I will love it. The thing I love most, Diary, is having a chat with my bed-bound mum, the woman who made me which will, without a doubt, make me cry. Love you, Mum, there, I've said it for today.

I'm glad I'm not in work today. It was a challenging place to be yesterday, especially as I'm not getting any sleep. It makes the prevalent tittle-tattle too difficult to deal with. I'm oversensitive

One Leg Out

and the little sarcastic comments I can usually brush aside broke me yesterday, and I wanted to hand in my notice. It's irrational behaviour from sleep deprivation because their silliness usually amuses me. Luckily, a couple of lovelies came to my aid and toughened me up. I even managed to knock a wing mirror clear off a parked van in the works car and managed to, somehow, blame the other driver for silly parking. Oops.

I will never understand the need for lady drama. It really is beyond me. I have always tried to look for the best in people, even the most bitter and awkward because no one's perfect, right? There is usually a reason, a back story. Even the most venomous person has some goodness, albeit buried deep. At work that theory goes out of the window. I have to squint hard to get a glimpse of nice, and I still struggle to see it. I will persevere. I have decided to win them over, fuckers.

Anyway, Diary, it's my birthday. It's my birthday, happy birthday to me! I have an update on the boy. His festival went well, he came back looking like he'd been stranded in the desert for a month and his clothes were dusty and stinking of smoke — he assured me it was not him. He was also in serious need of a bath. Ha, I don't think he'll go again anytime soon — yeay. The next worry for me is his driving. As I said before, for his imminent seventeenth birthday he wants to learn to drive, eek. Will I ever sleep with him at the wheel? It's a new kind of worry to look forward to. Wake up, son, I want my present.

Carla Day

Dear Diary.

Dressing Rooms and Tears

Not long ago, I seriously fell out with myself. I went to buy a new pair of jeans and wish I hadn't. Jeans are the one item I will spend money on. The fit of your jeans is important, we all a have different shapes and curves and the wrong jean could be a fatal fashion faux pas. I'm under no illusion, I don't look amazing in jeans because of my fat ass. The irony is, they brought in skinny fits just as I was no longer skinny. This is a shame because I would have killed that look a couple of years ago. However, I still wasn't prepared for the flagrant honesty of the mirror. Fuckidy fuck, I came out of the shop so depressed, I headed straight to Costa Coffee for a FULL FAT cortado and zingy lemon tart.

I came out of the shops with no jeans and a significant amount of self-loathing that needed an immediate sugar fix. Diary, the mirrors in M&S and Next are ridiculously big and every inch of my cellulite covered arse was lit up like a Christmas tree. Six pair of jeans, Diary, and not one of them fit. They were all size eighteen! How could this be? The jeans I have at home are a size sixteen, albeit tight. I must admit to myself that, perhaps, I'm not trying hard enough. I'm sure the woman in the next dressing booth to me chuckled when she heard a whimpering, 'For fuck sake,' from mine as my sixth pair of jeans rested on my thigh, refusing to budge any further. I have to say, at the time, I was so angry with myself that I just wanted to eat anything in sight because it seems even when you try, nothing happens and, well, oh, just fuck it all.

Then, I saw the error of my ways — after scarfing down my coffee and cake and decided to give it another go. Let's start again, Diary, eh?

Dear Diary,

Mothers and Sons

My birthday turned out to be spectacularly amazing and not because I did something dazzling, like a posh champers lunch, or a night at the theatre. It was more simplistic. I managed to get my son and dog out for a walk on the beach. I have been trying to coax him out of his technology and into the fresh air for some time. As it was my birthday, it seemed he couldn't refuse because I kind of made him feel guilty. Ah, what the hell, it was my day and if it takes bribery, so be it. Just to talk to him, because he had no other choice than to participate, was so lovely, I got my boy back for an entire afternoon, and we talked about everything from his college to my childhood. To see him running around the beach with our tiny dog-girl was such a beautiful sight. He acted silly and yet grown up at the same time. I managed to get a glimpse of the child before he disappears into manhood. My perfect day. The evening was gorgeous too. My fella cooked a nice dinner, and there was even a birthday cake. Surrounded by people I love, I was temporarily excused from my madness and felt normal, I didn't realise how un-normal I feel most of the time.

The work saga, Diary, continues to both amuse me and infuriate me. The waspishness of some of the ladies is bordering on sociopathic. There remains a consistent need for drama and try and drag you right into the middle of it, they will. I'm distancing myself from it all as much I can. I can't lie and say that I don't sometimes get a kick out of it, if it doesn't involve me, that is. But often your opinion will be asked even when it has nothing to do with you. When someone asks me, they will get an honest opinion and sometimes, oh my God, that is really not helpful to anybody because I find myself having verbal diarrhoea and I'm pretty sure that Chinese whispers will convey my words to something entirely different and I will find myself right in the sodding middle. How do you then unscramble that egg? The answer is by saying absolutely nothing, just listen, and nod, and if asked, say, 'I'm not sure,' and change the subject to baking or sex. Otherwise, the whole thing can get emotionally cancerous and grow into a particularly malignant merry-go-round.

Dear Diary.

What Day Is It?

I've lost count what day this is because I can't remember much of anything. I'm not in the mood for much today. I think it's because my partner upset me yesterday and because I'm a thinker, the feelings lingered. We always have a bit of ongoing banter about age-related crap — there's that phrase again — and weight and other nonsense, comments are thrown back and forth but are all innocent enough. Last night, however, I was hurt and offended and when I voiced that opinion, he seemed to think I was being over-reactive. The conversation went something like this:

Him: 'Your belly looks big today.' We were slobbed out on the sofa and my hand was under my top resting on my belly, so it did look like a bit of a first-trimester pregnancy bump.

Me: 'My hand is under my top. ' I give him a little stare, nothing nasty, just a friendly warning not to continue with the remarks because I'm sensitive and really mad with myself after sneaking a small tub of Ben & Jerry's ice cream before he came home from work.

Him: 'I wish you would go back to being skinny again.' Laughter.

Me: 'That was fucking insensitive.'

Him: 'You know we always have banter.' Laughs a bit more.

Me: 'That was too far.'

Him: 'Now you're looking for an argument.' Yes, I was because he had overstepped the mark.

Me: 'How can you say that?' My ball-breaking stare is more intense now.

Him: 'Stop it, it was a joke.' Laughter is fading.

Me: 'It didn't feel like a joke.'

Diary, my mood went from okay to really upset, and I think it was because I knew I was looking a bit, well, a lot swollen and felt uncomfortable and the fact it was pointed out made me feel shitty. There was no anger, just a huge dollop of selfloathing, so I took myself off to bed and put on my comfy fatpant pajamas. Maybe he was only joking, and we do have silly banter all the time. But because I knew he was spot on, it hurt.

Carla Day

The sun is shining and I'm usually up and out, but today I'm just annoyed with myself. I'm lethargic and my jeans feel tighter than ever, I need to start my diet once more. Even I'm sick of hearing it. Also, my dog is skinny, as if she's suddenly lost weight. I bathed her yesterday and could feel her ribs. I've been to the pet store today to buy her a different, more expensive variety of food and get her some nice doggy treats. I hope she isn't poorly. She has been whimpering a lot lately. I'll keep you posted. The thought of not having that little ray of light in my life is just too painful. She is my best friend and walking simply wouldn't be the same without her tiny shadow trotting behind me and her ears pricking to the sounds of my moaning. I'm being silly, perhaps it's just a belly ache. Please God, let it be that.

Update: girl dog is fine...

Dear Diary,

Funerals and Brain Fog

I'm restless. On today's visit to my weather-beaten log, it was cold and windy, so I didn't sit for long. I ambled along from beach to beach sniffing up the air that for some reason reminded me of home. It wasn't a sea smell, it was more reminiscent of the countryside, farm fields and summer rain. It made me think of my family all those miles away, and I really missed them. My mind won't calm, and I'm not sure for what reason.

I thought a walk in the fresh air and a think of how to organise my day would be a good start. I started to plan my day, as you do. "I'll go back and put a casserole in, then do the washing and get it ready for the weekend away." Yes — the Cotswold weekend has arrived and, no, I'm no lighter. I began planning which rooms I would tidy and what beds needed changing, ordinary stuff, when something extraordinary popped into my head. I wondered, bizarrely, what my funeral would be like.

Maybe it was the smell of home, taking me back to recent funerals of friends and family lost. It was the strangest thing, Diary. I thought about the type of music I would have — Delibes' Flower duet. There would be white fragrant gardenias, and everyone should wear white or cream. Why on earth would I think about that? I've been unsettled since and a bit spooked. I went for a smear test recently and perhaps subconsciously I'm wondering if something sinister is going to pop up, some sort of macabre news. I'm worried about my little dog losing weight. It could be just a random thought, but it's freaked me out all the same. Anyway, I've had a nice long bath and listened to Radio Four and learned that the box jellyfish has sixty anuses. I laughed so hard I farted in the bath. That cheered me up, Diary. It comes to something when the one place you go to for sanctuary conjures up images of death. Perhaps I'll walk somewhere else for a while.

Dear Diary,

I'm So Happy

I'm in a remarkably good mood. My shift at work was so pleasant I left the building smiling, and the day continues to be crisp and clear and bright. It's the sort of day that makes you want to eat a casserole and drink red wine, not that I need any encouragement. I was sent a picture, a dirty picture, on social media this morning, that has made me smile to myself all day and forward said picture to all my female friends, including my sister who was in an important meeting in Belgium.

Apparently, her colleagues found it amusing too. My friend's replies started off a bit of girlie banter, and I've been giggling all day because the picture showed a man's naked bits. It's silly really because I can't think of anything I'd rather not see, but the sight of it in the context it was sent, really, really tickled me.

Anyhow, Diary, I've made social progress, I have organised drinks with the neighbours next week — yes, the skinny marathon runner — and a night at the theatre to see the production of *Allo Allo* later in the month. Plans, Diary, I need stuff to look forward to. Even if I do convince myself that said stuff are targets to lose weight. Pfft. I haven't lost a single pound, not one. Size eighteen skinny fits just purchased. Oh, the irony. They should be called not so skinny fits for the slightly overweight, disillusioned fat asses.

I can't believe this is the very first year I haven't even carved a pumpkin, at least, for my house nor made an effort for a Bonfire Night. We even watched the neighbour's fireworks out of the bedroom window because we couldn't be bothered to go out. I think boredom and lack of funds has dampened our spirits. The Cotswolds weekend is this weekend, and I have it on good authority that bendy-wendy Frenchie is NOT coming. She is lovely, lovely, lovely. But a tiny bit of me is chuffed. I will be walking fourteen miles and taking in a small hill, not a mountain this time. I hope we have good weather. We have a meal booked for the evening which I'm looking forward to immensely.

My fella is *still* not getting any action. Poor bugger. This is despite me having a pep talk with myself almost every day.

"Come on, have a bath, be loving, make an effort, you are going to lose him, you stupid woman." Come nine o'clock, I'm dead to the world, snoring and can't think of anything less appealing than sex. Chuffing Hell! Maybe being in our camper will get me in the mood? It's funny how I can summon up a bit of debauchery when we are away.

Anyway, Diary, today is a bloody good day. I haven't had the urge to hit a single soul, not one.

Carla Day

Dear Diary.

Walking It Off

We have arrived at our Cotswold destination at a campsite neatly tucked away in a bowl of idyllic countryside. All of the surrounding villages look like they've been dipped in honey. I am happy, almost too happy, as if I've been injected with an extra dose of serotonin, which I believe is the correct word for the brain's happy juice. We cycled through a village earlier that was too pretty to describe, I seriously wouldn't do it justice. There was a smell of bonfire smoke as an old man burned leaves in the garden of his thatched cottage.

One Leg Out

Horses ran wild in a field and pheasants screeched in a paddock. It was a bright sunny day and I realised just how much we needed this break. I felt a weight lift today. I felt guilty that I'd said I didn't want Frenchie to come. I'm sad she isn't now because I will be with the boys and as lovely as they are, they don't do girlie conversation. I'll miss chatting with her on the walk. Come back, Frenchie, all is forgiven, you can even do the splits. We have made friends with a family of ducks that seem to like Bombay mix. They are hanging outside the camper van now nagging us for more and making a racket, perhaps we shouldn't have fed them? We — me and my fella — are getting on brilliantly and are all smiles and laughter. I had almost forgotten what it sounded like. That's what holidays are all about. Getting away, changing from the environment where normality resides. It all goes towards lifting your spirits and bonding and it might even end up in the bedroom. Wink, wink. My sister might even drive up with my mad family and join us for the evening meal.

Maybe it's because I've crossed the border and I feel at home that I feel so happy?

Carla Day

Dear Diary.

Red Coat

On my recent holiday I have been doing a lot of muddled thinking. As I ploughed through fields, farm lands, and plodded up hills and along the gloriously-muddy tracks of several, stunning valleys, I turned my mind to the past. I find it fascinating how the mind works and how selective it is of when it decides to pluck out a particular hidden memory.

A blood-red coat on a passing walker is what conjured up the image of a young girl I once knew. Her name was Samantha. When I was about nine-years-old, she turned up at our primary school in a tattered red coat. She was so quiet hardly anyone noticed her. She was skinnier than a heron's leg and pasty, the beautiful kind of pale you find on a typical English rose. She seemed quite serious, an unusually pretty girl. Her hair was shoulder-length, centre-parted, poker-straight and rich auburn. She had high cheekbones and naturally-pink rosebud lips, and her clothes smelled a bit fusty, like they'd just come out of a trunk, although her skin smelled soapy and her hair fresh-air clean. The essence of her is still part of my memories.

Samantha was from the local orphanage. The minute I clapped eyes on her melancholy face, I became curious and found her interesting, she was a sort of puzzle I knew I had to take under my wing. The shy girl was different, and I've always been drawn to what I consider different, because I've always felt different too. There was something about the world she was hiding behind her large hazel eyes. A world she never ever talked about. I presumed that world to be morose and possibly cryptically sad. I tend to do that. I read my own gloomy story into someone's life, even if I don't know the rumours in my head to be true. I don't know why, but with her I was scared to ask her about her past. Instinct, maybe? Or, perhaps, I didn't want to upset her when she already seemed so humble and somehow troubled.

She was a dreamy girl and seemed far away for a lot of the time. I used to visit her at the orphanage, and we would roam the grounds and hide from the staff. It was a beautiful rambling mansion, but to a young girl it was a very eerie place, and I'd imagined ghosts had lived there. She didn't seem very interested in food which I could never understand because I would eat anything put in front of me and still will. I would offer her food, but she would just turn her nose up and smile a watery, disengaging smile. Something in me wanted to fatten her up, perhaps she was happy as she was?

I invited her to my house, but she was on curfews, so I didn't get to see her as much as I wanted. I remember thinking when we were together that she didn't have a house that smelled of a roast dinner on Sundays, or a sister to argue with, or a mum to cuddle, or a dog to walk. I guess I used to feel sorry for her and wondered if it might be torturous for her being in a family environment?

Samantha had very few belongings, and the ones she did have she was so very possessive of. To her, it was obvious, each item was precious, looked after and very much appreciated. She would empty the items out of her bag quite often and count them to make sure they were all there. The only one of these items that sticks in my mind is a round plastic purse with a clasp which always had coins in. She would count them too. I'm not sure what happened to her, but I know she disappeared as quickly as she came, and we lost touch. I was quite sad when she left but as a child you just accept stuff. I have a lovely seventies-style photo of us wearing woolly hats, with red fingertips and noses, stood next to a snowman we built together at school. We look happy and freezing. For the whole walk I was thinking about her. Isn't that weird? I must try and find her.

I'll keep you posted, Diary.

Dear Diary.

Yeay

Thanks to the octopus arms of social media, I found my girl. It was an overwhelming experience. I don't know what I expected but when I knew she was happy, it was the first time I've felt genuine emotion for quite a while. It was a validation of sorts, for me, that I am indeed a human being with a fully functioning heart and an empathetic view, rather selfishly, it was a relief that I could feel at all. I was elated that I found her and when I saw her picture on Facebook, she was exactly the same, albeit now blonde. That same hauntingly beautiful face and big hazel eyes stared back at me and tears sprung into my eyes, it was Samantha.

She has a new surname, but that troubled look behind the eyes had all but disappeared, and she looked terribly happy. We have arranged to meet up next time I go back to my hometown. She was blown away at my description of that time and amazed at how insightful I was. I think her initial reaction was to be a bit afraid of revisiting her past. I detected a hesitant tone in her messages. Once she had rolled the thoughts around her head and processed my impromptu, very personal connection, she was elated too. One day she has promised to tell me her back story.

That will remain private though, Diary.

Carla Day

Dear Diary,

I Forget

I forget a lot these days. Bah, humbug.

Everywhere I go I'm surrounded by Christmas cheer. It's no good, every shop is reeling out ancient, festive tunes on this monotonous loop that is just unbearable. Why is the whole world so fucking cheerful? All the staff at work have asked me, at least once, 'Have you started yet?' I presume they mean Christmas shopping. I can't be bothered to explain it bores the shit out of me, all this smiley, seasonal, shopping-frenzy stuff, so I just say

One Leg Out

I'm a last-minute kind of girl.

This time of year, costs a fortune I just don't have, and it forces you into social situations you are not comfortable with. Well, I'm not but then you know my dilemma with people and the general intolerance of them, Diary. Bah, humbug. I'm not sure when I lost the magic of Christmas, it must have been gradual. It's certainly not the same since my grandparents passed away and my mum became bed-bound. But I think even before that I started to see it as a huge unnecessary expense and found all traditional values and wholesome good spirit seemed lost in greed and competitive buying.

As I could never afford the best gifts, I guess I couldn't compete, not that I wanted to. I would have been happy with a tangerine and nut-filled stocking, but it seems the world outgrew social importance, interaction, gatherings and closeness and opted for gluttony and being desirous of material things. Diary, the festivities and the fervent clamor of people in the shops stuffing their bags with materialistic crap, and the general happiness is winding me up a treat, and I can feel myself getting angry at Christmas.

I don't want to explode. Fortunately, it is also the time of year when alcohol is around in abundance, so I'll be okay. Can you believe I didn't really drink much at all until four years ago, at least not in a grown-up way? I would be merry after just one glass of fizz. Now, I can down a whole bottle of red and still walk in a straight line. I've tried it, it's true. I've grown up.

Carla Day

My boy is older, of course, so the mountain of presents he used to get under the tree has dwindled to driving lessons and a few gifts to open. Me and my partner don't buy for one another. We opted to save the money for a "nice" weekend away — I hate that word, nice — which always sounds like a great idea until we sit twiddling our thumbs of Christmas morning, wishing we had got a little something to open.

I guess the inner-child needs to tear off wrapping paper, which recalls a peculiar habit I had as a child. I used to sit for hours on my mum's kitchen floor peeling the labels off fizzy drinks bottles, I have no idea why. Random.

Anyway, I would like to feel festive and genuinely elicit some type of excitement and emotion, so I'm taking myself off to a castle where they have stalls selling local produce and unusual gifts, Christmas fare, carols, and mince pies. Perhaps it will get me in the mood? Maybe I'll even buy someone a present. I must buy a bottle of Harvey's Bristol to toast my grandma on Christmas Eve, it was her favourite tipple. In fact, I think it was the only liquid she would tolerate during her last days on earth. Maybe it made the thought of dying easier?

I hope there is a Christmas tree in the castle courtyard that is so tall it spikes right up into the night and is covered in soft white lights. I hope the band has a trumpet player, and I hope I can find Christmas and the joy I once knew from it. I do remember that joy, the little ball of excitement that lodges in your stomach as a child. The anticipation of fleeting magical visions that tips your senses over the edge, gorging on sumptuous foods that are indicative of those few special days. The dreams that nestle inside your head and keep you warm, the family mayhem that drives you nuts and the sheer chaotic happiness of it all. Maybe it's only when you are small and innocent that you feel these things?

Thanks again, Diary.

Carla Day

Books, Coffee, and Peace

After a recent trip to a coffee shop, I thought I'd share with my experience with you. I'm a modern, middle-aged woman wanting to go and have a nice cup of coffee and read a good book in relative peace and quiet. I've always loved that kind of oldie-worldly atmosphere and the smell of fresh coffee brewing. There's something homey about it, in a way you don't get at home.

Maybe it's the complete mixture of people at the tables and

the people watching I'm able to do in between paragraphs while my book says, "I'm busy. Please don't interact with me." I like to try and get a sofa if I can, so I can semi-lounge as I savor the bittersweet coffee and drink in lovely words. I was all prepared for an hour of luxurious selfishness to absorb myself in someone else's world. I ordered my coffee, clutching my book under my arm and scanning the area for a good seat. I noticed most of the people in there were all staring at some kind of device. One bloke in a suit, sipping on an Americano, was tapping away at his laptop and talking to someone on his phone with a thin moustache of frothy milk on his top lip. Most people in there — both with company and alone — were looking at some kind of screen. *Thank God I've brought my phone*, I thought.

Diary, it was a shock. I know that we all use our devices all the time, but I honestly thought this little sanctuary might have escaped that particular progression. It seems not. I slouched on my overly slouchy sofa and got my book out as the woman next to me tapped furiously at her screen, shaking her head at something and her nails were clicking on the glass in a very irritating way, I dread to think what the receiver of the text was getting. I blinked away the thought, and opened my book on page fifty-seven, wriggled myself comfortable, and began to read. The coffee was just how I like it, strong and short.

I kept reading the same line over because a man who smelled very potently of aftershave and his girlfriend sat right next to me on a small round table, and they were discussing a post of

Carla Day

Facebook that made them laugh. They played the GIF post very loudly, and I coughed my annoyance at them and peered at them over my glasses, like my grandma used to when she was mad. What can you say about it though? It's not a library after all. I could not concentrate for all the tea in China. I think I should start a hunt for a nice quiet, back-street bookshop where nobody bothers you.

Costa Coffee, Diary, was a complete hive of activity and I soon pulled my phone out of my bag to check my Facebook messages, just like everyone else. I suppose it's a sign of times. I miss the old days.

Dear Diary,

What a Load of Crap

Here are today's musings...I was listening to the radio earlier, where a group of women were talking about celebrating the menopause. I found myself saying, 'Pffa.' I can understand that we should be celebrating the milestone of where we have reached in life as women, but celebrating the menopause? In the words of Churchill—not the marvellous wartime prime minister—but the ever-cheerful nodding Bulldog: No, no, no! That dreadful, dirty, M word and all it entails spells out misery, to me at least. We should be applauding ourselves for being physically and mentally tormented? What!

Diary, I will brush aside my sweaty blanket and laugh in the face of my receding hairline and stick two fingers up at my eternal insomnia. I will embrace the exhaustion and dance at the thought of my brain fog and dry mouth. I think not. I can't bring myself to do it.

Since the untimely, formative part of my perimenopausal diagnoses, my life has been a living Hell. So, I won't be joining that celebration. However, I can see what they mean. It is a real achievement to have successfully made it to middle age without cracking up. Especially when you take into consideration perpetual relationship turmoils, childbirth, parenting, and general premenstrual insanity which graces most women once a month for an entire shitty week — perhaps that's a taste of what's to come, nature's way of saying, 'Well, you think this is bad wait till the big M!'

And to think of all those women who started the perilous menopausal journey way before their time, that's just some cruel twist of fate. Thank the Lord — pardon the pun — I'm a humanist rather than a religious person, or I would be cursing this perverse so-called God for being so bitterly cruel. Even worse, can you imagine the torment of those poor women who started the menopause before having borne a child? How excruciating that must be, what quagmire of emotions for them, eh, Diary?

I am a proud raconteur of my menopause experience, a creator of my own story and what it means to me. My travels with the

One Leg Out

menopause, Dearest Diary, have taken me down a long, hard road, and yet there is no end in sight. Thank goodness for you.

I've joined a group of women on a closed group in an online forum who help one another to get through the-funny-farmyears, to see if perhaps I can gain anything from it. I'll let you know. I am having a one to one with a mentor soon to see what guidance I might need for a nutritious and healthy lifestyle. You know the type of thing, thoughts on my well-being and so on. Perhaps she will convert me to Epicureanism and send me in the direction of the Greek philosopher Epicurus whose philosophy said, 'We should not fear death but find happiness in life.' Something like that, anyway. Let's see if my mentor can kick my enormous, can't-be-arsed-to-do-anything butt into shape.

We must celebrate some things, I suppose, like, what our bodies and minds as women have been through and accomplished. I have given birth to a child and gained the glorious stretch marks to show that I have been a woman in all that she is meant to be, that's fucking amazing. I have raised a child who was both incredibly beautiful and often emotionally difficult. I have loved many people, and I have mourned a few too. I have held the hands of a person who is dying. I have looked into the eyes of a brand-new soul. I have seen happiness and wondrous things with my eyes, and I have felt the deepest pain and been at times severely depressed. I have climbed mountains and contemplated life on their summits. I have been loved and cherished. I have given a lot of myself to others. I've been empathetic and selfish. I have felt all that life has to offer.

Yes, Diary, when I look at it like that, those things are pretty damned astonishing in their simplicity. I'll celebrate that.

P.S. Diary, my smear test results came back ok, I'm not dying, after all, and there have been no more thoughts of my own funeral. I have been busy lately, and my trip to the theatre was so funny. I had one too many and had the hangover from Hell the following morning, but it was all in the name of sanity. The show was hilarious, and the night out such a much needed tonic. My greed for alcohol consumption was so much so that I seemed to siphon it out of the glass in record time. I spent the second act desperately wanting to pee, but I was stuck in the middle of the row. My, your bladder can't half burn when it's full of gin, wine, and more gin. I made a rule never to mix my drinks, I must have forgotten … ha.

One Leg Out

Dear Diary,

Tears for Fears

Another dog walk has brought to my attention the fact that I am still an emotional wreck. I have been off HRT for several weeks now and I am, at least, clear of my crankiness. However, the pitfalls are: weight gain, idleness which I believe is entirely my fault, and emotional stupid-ness. I am crying at silly things. An ambulance, Diary, yes, you heard right. I heard once that in other countries, vehicles don't move out of the way when an ambulance is approaching, even when it's blue-lighting. I find it somehow very special when everyone pulls over to make way for

Carla Day

what might be a potential life and death situation.

It happened to me today, and I was so tearful and found myself wishing that person a speedy journey to the hospital and desperately hoping for their recovery. The person may well have just had a broken leg, but I always imagine the worst. To top that, shortly after, a moving song came on that remained me of a friendship I lost, and I thought about that person and randomly bawled my eyes out. I thought I had dealt with that, it seems not.

Anyway, the emotional wave will pass, I'm sure. They always do. The sensitiveness follows a wonderful day out with family at a mansion where a Christmas choir singing so beautifully brought tears to my eyes — no surprise there, then. It made me feel a bit oversensitive, which of course I am at present, but why was nobody else emotional? It was a very touching moment, a crescendo of angels' voices — no, just me, then. It was a lovely decent-sized fair with delightful festive gifts and the perfunctory food vans wafting gorgeous smells throughout the courtyard. It was also very muddy and bitterly cold, but still, the atmosphere gave me a little flicker of excitement for Christmas, even though I am still bigger than I wanted to be for the visit home. Hey ho … Off to Oxford I go!

Oh, I forgot my nephew's ninth birthday. How is that possible? He is one of the most important people in my life. I think about him and my other little nephews all the time. How on earth did I forget? I'm losing my marbles, they are rolling off the pavement and down the road to God knows where. Good job I can laugh at it. I'm going to have to spoil him at Christmas. There was a little bookstore at the castle, where you donate money and take a few books. I found six that I fancied reading, including another copy of *The Tiger's Wife*, an absolute addiction and favourite. My partner asked, 'Why do you need another copy?' I replied, 'I love this author's work, you can never have enough Tea Ochrecht.' It sounded silly even to me, but that book is awesome, and I do impulsive things lately that make no sense, even to me. Anyhow, I didn't buy a single gift but came home with an armful of reading material. I was made up.

The intimacy in my relationship is returning, albeit slowly. It's kind of like a thing you think about a lot. In your mind it happens one way, but the reality of the menopause makes it more difficult. You have to have a fair amount of lubricant to hand no matter how desirous you might be of your partner. Anyway, my love life's coming back. My partner's ecstatic and may even decorate the hall if I keep up the good work. Oh, that did make me laugh.

Life at the moment, Diary, is looking up. I don't know why. I can't really give you exact reasons, but I feel cheerful, hopeful for something positive happening. As my moods seem to fluctuate, ask me again tomorrow, I might well be fed up again because the bloody menopause seems to dictate my entire life. I'm still waiting for my one-to-one with my menopause coach, who I'm positive is going to tell me to eat well, a healthy nutritional diet, and to do more exercise. Things I already know, I do know them, inside out, so why does it take a total stranger to drum up a bit of enthusiasm for my own well-being?

Gawd knows, Diary, but I will work it out.

Dear Diary,

Getting Old

The sun was at its brightest today, a huge ball of energetic sunlight dominated the sky. It was so big and blazing it made me shield my eyes and look to the ground which was a good thing because the sun had melted the frost, and the path was sludgy and slippery and full of long snake tracks where bikes had raced through earlier.

The light was typically wintery and almost too white-gold to look at directly, but I really wanted to. Even with good sunglasses perched on my nose, it was too much. But the colours it made across the water and to the hedgerows created all kinds of yellow. I sat for a few minutes on my special weather-beaten log, but my backside was too cold, so I carried on, my eyes fixed on the glowing volume of water and the birds silhouetted on the surface, just bobbing about. There were young ones too and that made me think of growing up. As you well know by now, Diary, it doesn't take much to set my mind off, wondering about things.

Today it was about growing up. Growing up is hard to do — that song came into my head. I don't think we really do ever grow up. I don't even know if such a thing exists? I think we age and are expected to act according to our age but really most of the changes are superficial and on the outside. Most old people you ask say they feel no different to when they were young. They have the same emotions and feelings they always did but their outer shell alters beyond recognition, it becomes chipped and worn thin. Maybe that's why I love old people so much because of their young stories, mischievous eyes, and the attachment to life. Their tales of the past and the perpetual connection to youth appeals to my weird side which fears dying.

I have always been afraid of dying itself but not death that follows when your mind no longer thinks. That might sound strange, but I imagine dying to be like a ginormous panic attack, and of course, I have them often. I imagine the mind stays alive well after your heart stops beating, and the body is too knackered to keep functioning, and the mind just wants you to breathe and talk, but of course, you are dead, so you can't. What a nightmare, that thought terrifies me. Can you imagine wanting to so desperately say those last words, but you can't because you feel yourself slipping away? It must be very silent and scary. Ignore me, I do get maudlin, Diary.

Anyway, as for growing old, maybe we do mature a little, because we feel we have to be more responsible and be the pioneers and good examples for next generation, give them someone to look up to. It's hard being a grown-up, especially when you still feel like a kid. I often feel like a fraud because I'm still working stuff out now and having tantrums, even more so since the menopause started. How on earth did I manage to raise a child when I still go to bed with a blankie and a hot chocolate, and I like the odd cuddle with my teddy? My conclusion is: "grown up" is something we invented to create a safe space for children to imagine, a future place where things will eventually make sense, and you will have wrinkles, but all your childhood will come together here in grown-up-dom. Of course, it was all a big fat lie because not all of it does make sense, not really. I'm still waiting to feel grown up.

Dear Diary,

Get Ready for a Misery Dump

Nothing feels right today, I'm unhappy with practically everything about me. This is an altogether new level of misery. I woke up depressed. Before I'd even opened my eyes, I felt the weight of the world pressing me to the bed. I woke at 6.30 a.m. of course, sweaty and exhausted, and I binge-watched a series I'm into until twelve p.m. in bed. Apart from the fifteen minutes when I rolled out of bed and into my car with an oversized scarf wrapped around my dressing gown to disguise the fact I'm wearing one. Then I drove to McDonald's and got myself a breakfast and a coffee and went back to bed with my grey cloud.

I'm depressed because I'm angry, angry that I'm not fighting harder to beat this thing. It's the flab on my middle and the cellulite on my arms, my receding gums, my big face, blah, blah, blah. My situation is just a big fucking headache. I watched TV in a sweaty mess until I could stand the stickiness no more. I showered at midday. I straightened my hair, made my eyes up trying not to look down to the pile of blancmange with nipples, drying my hair in the nude because I'm sweating like roasting pork and can't stand anything against my skin. Fuck-a-doodledoo.

Even after painting my toe and fingernails, I felt like crap and forced myself out for a walk, fearing another eight hours stuck to the bed watching *Suits* — Harvey Specter is seriously fit.

I'm sure I'm turning into Miss Trenchbull. As I cornered a gravelled path and turned toward the lake, I'm sure even the pair of swans gliding across the water looked the other way. The loudness of the gravel crunching beneath my feet irritated me. I was positive it was only so loud because of my weight. I thundered around the pond with a dark cloud hanging over my head and back along the seafront with a bee in my bonnet about life's unfairness.

I think I transferred my misery to my dog who whenever I looked back was sitting on a tuft of grass looking totally fed up and not willing to move. She senses when I'm moody and keeps away. Even the weather was depressed and indecisive, oneminute sunshine, one-minute cloud and drizzle. The only positive was a rainbow, a perfect arc of colour over the seaside houses. I had to force myself to do the whole hour's walk because I kept making excuses to myself to stop and go back to the car. 'It's too cold, it's too windy, it's too wet.' I didn't enjoy my jaunt until I had almost finished the route.

I have this inexplicable need to be severely depressed before I kick my own butt to do something. It's a vicious circle that I have wriggled myself into. If only I could break it once and for all. There are things I could do. I know them all, which brings me to my next question, Diary. Is slowing metabolism responsible for my weight gain? I've thought long and hard about this. I don't think it's entirely to blame.

The reduction in estrogens does slow it down, but body composition during the menopause means more fat and less muscle and muscle cells burn more fuel. Our calorie burning engine becomes slowly defunct, so we need to step up and do more exercise and eat better. That's what it all boils down to, Diary, but fuck, it's hard to keep up with the fat. I think that coaching session might come in handy after all.

Dear Diary

Fuck I'm Tired

I've been so topsy turvy lately. I haven't even the energy to talk to you. Lethargy has wiped the floor with me. I've held in my woes until today when my melancholy mood has urged me to consult you about something important.

Last night, as I lay in my sweat-soaked bed having an emotional breakdown about life and again the unfairness of it, I had a missed call from my sister, then another. I knew instantly that something was wrong. I'd been in turmoil all day, feeling restless, sensitive, and generally sad and angry at the same time. I'm not

Carla Day

sure if the universe was messaging me with subliminal pulses of sadness, but instinctively, I knew that somewhere, something had happened but thought it was just me being menopausal and unduly weird.

I had cried on and off all day and argued and fought with my partner, until I gave up and went to bed with a large glass of red wine and a big dollop of self-pity. I thought the missed call was about my mum. I thought there was bad news.

My sister knew my angst and before I had a chance to ask, she assured me it's not Mum, but there is bad news. It's Grandad, he passed away about an hour ago.' I suddenly felt relief and then had a little cry because he was the last remaining grandparent, and the blow of losing my other grandparents only a couple of years before was a situation I didn't deal with well.

I also felt massively guilty for not feeling sadder, convincing myself that ninety-seven was a ripe old age, and he'd had a wonderful and rich life. Should I feel that way? Should I not be more inconsolable? I cried more for me than for the loss of my dear blue-eyed grandad who was so full of spirit, warmth, and wisdom because he was such a wonderful person. That guilt made me feel selfish because I wept like a baby for my other three and mourn them still. Maybe the first sting was the worst and has prepared me for this loss. My highly emotional, menopausal state has made me overthink everything, even this. The simple fact that someone has died, and I cried, I am analysing to death — pardon the pun. I think too much. I don't have a dormant part of my brain, it works overtime and then some, all of my cogs clicking away 24/7. I have conversations with myself:

'Why did you cry just now?'

'Because I feel sad about my grandad,' I lie to myself.

'You sure it's not because you are relieved it's not Mum?'

'Well, it is that too, is that bad?'

'I don't know, I'm not sure what's acceptable but I think it's okay.'

'I must be a bad person?'

'No, I don't think so, its normal to think that, it's okay.'

Then, I cry because it's a relief to find I'm not horrible after all. I exhaust me.

I think a lot of my conflicting conversations with me are to do with the fact I'm so bloody tired. Every night, I'm back to one leg out. I'm hot, cold, warm, sweaty, and then freezing. I'm so confused, and it's bound to have an effect on my daytime cerebral function. Basically, I'm living in a zombie zone, a headspace full of ethereal fluffiness and nuanced daydreams, and I don't make sense, not even to me. I wander about mumbling and yawning and dreading the night because I will have to do the hokey cokey all over again. Do I give in? Do I go for more HRT and be in a consistent evil mood? Should I try phytoestrogens or bioidentical creams, natural supplements with very mixed reviews?

I'm ready to try anything at this point, Diary, anything at all. My one-to-one coaching is now postponed until the New Year, and I need to get through the festivities in one piece first. Then, I seriously have to tackle my mental and physical state, my crisis has gone way beyond talking to you about, I need to do something drastic.

It's two weeks to Christmas and now I have a funeral and a family Christmas to contend with. I'm still a plus size and still depressed about it as the whole family will be there. I'm very much wanting to find a hole to crawl into until the menopause has passed and I'm me again and smiling like I used to with genuine ease and uncomplicated thinking.

I think that's a way off yet but I'm sure as hell going to try and do something to manage this mess. On the plus side, Diary, tonight I'm making bread and butter pudding with extra currants, great comfort food that will not aid my weight loss. However, it will give me the sense of contentment one needs when their grandad has passed away peacefully in his sleep. God bless and sleep tight. I know, Diary, I'm an atheist but still feel like I should say it because he wasn't.

Update – at the funeral I find out he was an atheist. Go Grandad! Who knew?

Dear Diary,

Sex - To Have or Not to Have?

I swapped my weather-beaten log today for a giant boulder which had great views across the estuary. Winter sunshine is spectacular around this time of year and the piercing light gives such an ethereal feel to the day. I thought a lot again today about the man's role in the menopause, mainly because there was a couple who seemed middle-aged walking their giant poodle. They were quietly arguing about something, and he looked thoroughly fed up. It made me think about how my fella feels about this whole situation.

Carla Day

I know he becomes desperate because the main question he asks, when I'm seriously on one, is, 'How long will this thing last?' Meaning the menopause. My reply is usually, 'If you try understanding me more, we can get through this thing together more comfortably.' After which, I'll look at him with big eyes. Of course, the main theme is centred on sex and how much of it we are having. For a man, it must be pretty sad to feel constant rejection. I know that when my libido started to disintegrate, I felt sadness, a loss of sorts for both of us. I wanted him to understand that I still saw him exactly as I always have. Diary, I desire, fancy, and find him physically attractive. In fact, he is my perfect partner, but my body isn't working in tandem with my brain.

I have all the emotions that were there before, but my body doesn't seem to want to catch up with my emotions, and when it does, the physical symptoms make it either totally embarrassing because you are a sweaty mess and don't want to be touched or impossible because of the pain. It's a very strange thing and must be incredibly difficult to understand. I suppose for a man two and two makes four.

'If you are saying no to my advances, it must mean that you've stopped fancying me.'

It's not that simple, guys, it really isn't. There are things you can do, of course, Diary, to help alleviate certain problems like vaginal dryness. There are lubricants galore and a good vibrator is a must. Affection mustn't dry up either from both sides.

Effort should be made to cuddle and kiss your partner to make him or her feel loved, and I think that's what it's all about? I tried to explain to my partner that for me to have intercourse can be painful. I also explained that the edge of my vulva can feel as if there are a thousand tiny paper cuts around it and to penetrate beyond there actually brings tears to my eyes.

It's all about balance and finding other ways to keep our sex life healthy. So, we have invented new ways to entertain ourselves, Diary. I do, sometimes, make the effort even when I'm not really in the mood because I love my partner. He's suffering too, and I wonder how I would feel if he turned away from me when I came close to him. It would be awful, truly awful.

So, not only do we have to think about how on earth we are going to get through this, we must consider those around us too.

Neurotic warriors, we women are, eh, Diary?

Carla Day

Dear Diary,

Fat as ****

I've been shopping for a funeral outfit today, that little black dress. The idea was a big mistake. Not only am I larger than ever, I happen to have acquired new, deeper, more defined wrinkles which showed up beautifully under the brilliantly white lights of the dressing cubicles in all the major retailer stores I visited.

Initially, I didn't find a single thing that fit well, another reminder that I need to do something about my spiralling weight, because applying a little black dress to a "wholesome" figure just

One Leg Out

looks wrong. The added burden of looking absolutely ridiculous in front of the whole clan is giving me a serious headache. To make things worse, I am not only having hot flashes, but they have stretched out to one long sweat-fest. I am soaked for most of the day and when I'm not, I'm either in a rare, deep slumber, or in the shower. I'm always wet, clammy, and for some reason, sticky like glue is oozing from my pores. I am getting used to this feeling. It's as though I am transitioning into another being all together — a rather wet, miserable one. I have said "fuck" an awful lot today and with no remorse whatsoever.

I tried on a series of snug dresses, just below the knee which is, I believe, the acceptable hem length for funerals, and I couldn't breathe, every single lump showed up. The cellulite on my arms was so dazzlingly ugly, I quickly threw a cardigan on, so I didn't have to look at it. Even I couldn't stomach the sight of my arms because they are the reality of my laziness.

I don't have any desire to look like an egg-on-legs but I'm seriously struggling to find a style that hides the myriad of lumps I seem to have acquired of late. Fuck it, fuck it, fuck it! Well, as I marched away from the shopping park, almost in tears, I remembered my love of vintage clothes and took a route to the area that is full of charity shops.

In the very first store, I spotted a dress an M&S black number still with the label on, in a size sixteen. It looked roomy enough. I prayed it would fit — because I'm currently an eighteen in most things — as it was ideal, albeit a tad short. I became immediately happy because I had that this-is-gonna-look-good feeling. I hate the taboo surrounding second hand stuff, I've always loved it.

Diary, it fit like a dream, and I was so chuffed I said quietly, 'Fucking, yes,' While giving a little fist-pump to the mirror. I didn't even care who was listening. I carried on throughout the town centre, with a bit if a swagger on and came across a pair of vintage leather gloves, a cool scarf and a black-rose broach — which could be considered grandma-ish, but we will be at a funeral after all.

I began to smile because not only had I found a decent outfit but the whole thing cost fewer than twenty quid, and I was made up. I was about to celebrate with a Costa coffee but thought against the idea as it would definitely involve cake, so I held my head up high, Diary, and stomped past, sniffing up spiced lattes and warm cake.

The town was bustling and too busy for my liking, so I got out of there, sharpish. I drove home listening to some very nostalgic tunes, Dean Martin and his crooners sang, 'You're nobody till Somebody Loves You,' with such velvety voices and soft words that filled the small space in my car and brought a lump to my throat, I'm not quite sure why. Well, I have an idea it's possibly hormonal, all my sensitivity, but the song and the words didn't help matters much either.

I thought of my recently deceased grandad and wondered, why the Hell I am so preoccupied with what I'm going to look like when I'm supposed to be mourning? It's a strange old life, Diary, but today's successful trip made it a somewhat jubilantly strange day.

I've found from previous experience that grief strikes me in random spikes. I call them spikes because they are sharp, quick, and painful bouts of pain, often a complete surprise set off by music or word association or a sight, as if someone's literally stuck a knife into my heart and it really hurts and the sadness is suddenly unbearable. I might not be grieving my grandad right now, but I know my spirit well and know the grief is being stored away for my own protection. One day, when I'm somewhere in the future it will catch up with me, and I'll have a good cry and remember my grandad's beautiful nature and gentle ways and I'll miss him. Then my grieving will feel real and might engulf me for a while, it's just how it presents itself to me. I can't grieve on demand. I might not even cry at the time of the news, but grief catches up with me at will. My mind has its own way of dealing with stuff. For now, though, I'm handling it okay.

I just pray that my hair and make-up go according to plan at the funeral, Diary, because I have it all sorted in my mind. I know how I will style my hair and have a colour scheme in mind for my eyes that will make them pop rather than look menopausal piggy small.

Let's hope it doesn't rain and that I feel good about myself, or Christmas will be ruined all because I didn't get my arse into gear and drop that dress size, as I had intended. It should all be about family, sharing, caring, and spending quality time with loved

Carla Day

ones. But, I still care about how I look, Diary, is that silly?

One Leg Out

Dear Diary.

Scary

Last week, my son had an attack, a hemiplegic migraine. It's quite terrifying because he has the same symptoms as if he were having a stroke. Numbness rendered one side useless, and his speech became slurred. To follow that came a blinding migraine which lasted for a whole day. It is the second major one, he seems to get them once or twice a year. If that wasn't enough, he temporarily lost sight in one of his eyes. I'm sure it's as painful to watch as it is to have them, for a mother anyway.

Carla Day

There is nothing you can do apart from leave him sleep it off in a dark room and give him painkillers. It makes me cry to see him like this. I'm so glad they are bringing out a kind of EpiPen for migraine sufferers next year.

My boy also has hit party season and is spending time at house parties. It's a funny age, seventeen, not yet old enough for the pub but too old to hang about on the streets and in parks. House parties fill the gap. I dropped him off at one only last night, and I swear, the girls waiting outside were like mannequins, perfect specimens with long silky hair, flawless make-up and legs that belonged to a giraffe, and the skirts — so short! I looked away in case I got a glimpse of something I wasn't supposed to see. I'm sure it's the first time I saw him flustered, and I was sort of gushy with him because he's turning into a man. It's so amazing to watch him grow into an adult and do what young men are made to do. He is such a lovely boy. He better choose wisely, a girl that loves him as much as I do, ha. I bet he will go with his eyes, all boys do until they wise up and see beyond flesh and pretty eyes. Anyway, he stayed out at said party, and I've not heard from him yet and it's the afternoon.

Why do boys not call their mothers?

It's a rainy day today, the rain was soothing. I let it soak my face, it was so refreshing, and I didn't care that people were looking as I smiled up to the rain outside Tesco. It's just nice to feel cool, ha. It's a peaceful day because I'm at work and it's relaxing. Everything's chilled and it's cosy and warm and there is an endless vat of tea and a mountain of comforting Christmas snacks are on offer. I feel generally good, considering I slept for all of two hours last night. It's okay because that's become the norm. I don't know how I function at all if I'm honest, but I just do. I've noticed dark rings under my eyes though, which is a first. Work is calming down a bit. There seems to be a lull in the bitchy department, so I'm enjoying the temporary — it always is — serenity.

Grandad's funeral is this week, so I have decided to embrace my new fuller figure and go kick ass. I'm going to enjoy my family and not linger on my weight or any other negativity that's festered around me. I'm going to have a good Christmas and celebrate my grandad's wonderful life.

Dear Diary.

A Break from Men?

A friend not so long ago asked me what the menopause was like. She asked if I could describe it. She also asked if the menopause meant a break from men which I found hilarious because in part, it's true. A break from men is spot on because dealing with partners and their eternal hard-ons when you feel like you're dying can be tiresome, and yes, you do want a break from them. My response to her question wasn't instant. I tried to find an analogy that would give a better visual than the usual way of explaining it with dry vaginas, swollen vulvas, etc. It's a tough entity to describe. I finally, after much deliberation, came up with this:

Me: 'Imagine you are an apple.' She looked at me funny, as if she smelled bad feet.

Her: 'Go on.'

Me: 'Imagine without warning, someone inserts a straw into your core and begins to suck out your juice, so slowly you know something's not right but you can't say exactly what it is but you feel decidedly odd.'

Her: 'Okay.' She closed her eyes and wriggled in her seat which made me chuckle.

Me: 'Then, imagine your skin starts to pucker and becomes wrinkled and dry and your colour begins to fade.'

Her: 'Nice,' she says still with her eyes closed and her nose wrinkled.

Me: 'Now, imagine that your shape changes, lumps form, and you're so damned thirsty because you are being drained of fluids and hormones and you feel exhausted because you are desperately trying to feel like the apple you once were.'

Her: 'Sounds horrible, poor apple.'

Me: 'Okay, so now you are misshapen and swollen in parts, you are drying out and your inner core doesn't feel as strong as it once did. The chances your seedlings will survive to reproduce are practical nil. On top of all that, someone lights a match under you, so you sweat out even more moisture which causes all kinds of additional problems.'

Her: 'Please don't say there's more.'

Me: 'That's just the beginning, you become more and more withered, and your apple mind becomes affected because you are so exhausted just trying to be a normal apple in a barrel of other normal apples. They look a whole deal better than you and you just aren't the same, and you have increased chances of being thrown out of the barrel because you're not ripe enough to make cider anymore.'

Her: 'Sounds shitty. How do you cope being a misshapen, withered apple?' she asks, smiling but looking horrified too.

Me: 'You have no choice but to learn to manage it and hope you don't get thrown out.'

Her: 'God, I had no idea.'

Me: 'No, you really don't.'

Diary, it was a queer conversation really, but it made me think about how uninformed we apples really are.

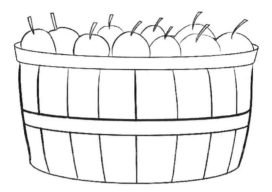

Dear Diary,

Death

I am seeing a lot about loss on social media at the minute, and the huge impact it has on loved ones left behind. Diary, one of our biggest fears is losing someone we love, and to do so at a time when we are all geared up to celebrate and share the festive season with family and friends is more than sad, it's a devastating blow that creates a cavernous space.

It's also the beginning of a long and difficult grieving period. As you know, Diary, this year I am heading home myself to one less loved one sat around the family Christmas table. I feel a huge amount of empathy for anyone experiencing loss, Diary, because I know only too well the ramifications that follow as your brain begins the complicated process of sorting how a human being who only yesterday was tangible and huggable is no longer on earth.

You suddenly find yourself relying on memories to see their face and hear their voice. It's a funny business, grief, an absurdly ethereal time and a very personal experience which everyone deals with in their own unique way and, Diary, I've had my issues with it.

Loss makes you question everything over the months following a loss, mortality, spirituality, religion, and you find yourself asking, what comes next, where do our loved ones go? There is a part of you that grapples with all your past beliefs because at the time of "death impact," you would dare to believe anything, just to feel close to them again.

Being an atheist, I struggled and got myself into a right old tangle. I even considered Christianity, just in case my loved ones were tucked away in some pocket waiting for me to believe, and I had been wrong in my values all this time. I wanted to believe because I was so desperate to feel them near again.

It took months of sitting in remote churches, talking nonsense to myself and wishing desperately for them to give me a sign they were okay, but of course, after I had grieved for long enough and tousled with my inner emotions, I went back to being an atheist.

I chose to believe that their electric pulses survived and are milling around somewhere in space and time. I can't really say I ever got over those losses that plagued me for a while, but I can say that I am changed because of them and the void remains. Diary, I would say to anyone experiencing loss at this time of year, or any other, 'May your sadness be brief, your memories long, and the love in your heart strong, always.'

Carla Day

Dear Diary,

Wet as An Otter's Pocket

Well, Diary, I lost the will to live a couple of days ago. Not literally, but I'd had enough by twelve o'clock when I was dripping beads of sweat into my coffee after a mortifying Tesco fiasco which I'll get to. I instantly gave up on my quest to go natural and sped to the doctors fully prepared to beg for HRT. Gradually, over the past three months, I've become worse and worse and looking more and more like a drowned rat. I was so tired and so irritable and not wanting to leave the house at all because I was too sweaty-looking and felt diseased.

One Leg Out

After food or drink consumption, the sweat-fest was so bad, I didn't want to eat out or have a hot drink. It was practically all day and night that I was wet and clammy. I picked up my emergency prescription that night.

The final straw was a morning in the shops, picking up last minute gifts for Christmas which almost cleared me out. Somehow, I ended up a blathering mess in Tesco. I went to one of those machines to get a photo printed out. It was one of those where you can Bluetooth your picture. All was well, Diary, until I squinted at the screen and patted my head which is where my glasses usually live only to find I'd forgotten them. A woman spotted my frustration and came rushing over. She asked, 'Do you need assistance?' Her tone wasn't friendly, more impatient. She could see the queue forming behind me, and I could clearly hear huffs and puffs at my slowness and daren't turn around. I began to sweat profusely, and the woman, who looked a bit Hitler-ish, stared at my shiny forehead, making me uncomfortable and stressed, so I sweated even more. I tore off my coat and started fanning my scarlet-glowing face with a leaflet, while she helped do things with my phone and locate the photo I needed. I explained to the woman, 'I'm really sorry, I forgot my glasses, otherwise, I would have done it myself.' She gave me quite an annoyed look as her lips curled into a smirk which made me feel terrible and really embarrassed. I drove to the doctor's immediately afterwards with tears in my eyes, feeling useless, old, and just wanting to die.

That, Diary, was the last time I'm going to feel like that. I know it will take time but if I don't manage this thing and take control, it's going to swallow me whole and digest me until I'm nothing but mush. Ah, that's better!

Dear Diary,

What Was All the Fuss About?

Driving home for Christmas — I was accompanied by that song about three times — along with a multitude of bell chiming carols. It was a long but serene journey. After all my trepidations, I started the day on a very positive note. I didn't have a meltdown while getting ready, nor did I contemplate staying put and cancelling the much-dreaded family celebrations. I slapped on my war paint and rode off to battle with my window down slightly while navigating the unexpectedly empty motorway, much to the annoyance of my son. The journey was dreamy, even though I was heading straight for a funeral and crowds of people appropriately dressed-to-the-nines in morbid black. I didn't feel sad.

I felt festive and merry and all those jovial things I had been waiting to feel suddenly overwhelmed me, and I realised how much I'd missed my lot. The very apparent sweat on my upper lip didn't faze me one bit. As you know, I'd been to the doctor the week before and begged her to let me go back onto HRT — which she did after BP checks — because I couldn't take those abominable symptoms a moment longer. Although it was early days, I felt positive I'd made the move and knew that within a week or so, I would be perspiration free and would endeavour to get a good night's kip.

The fact I hadn't lost a single pound I chose to ignore because if I'd acknowledged my lack of self-control and will-power, I wouldn't have gone. It was strange pulling up outside Mum and Dad's. Even though it's only Dad there now, I can't bring myself to say Dad's. It was a place I lived as a child and once believed in Father Christmas and elves and magic, and my heart ached for those long-ago times when the world seemed easier, even for me, the anxious child.

Inside the red-brick house my dad was waiting, and I wasn't sure what to expect, tears or the same laughter and lighthearted, childlike fun I'd always known. He had lost his father and of course, recent years had made us all a bit weaker, sensitive to loss, and more sentimental.

Diary, I found him to be just as he always was, strong and eager to show me fun things on TV. He launched into his usual patter, and we talked as we always had about things we always had. It was nice to be home, but I sensed he was being brave.

The funeral was, as I expected, full of people I knew I must see but wasn't yet ready to. I put on my bravest face, Diary, and cried at the kind words of the humanist preacher. It turns out I was wrong about my grandad, he was an atheist just like me and the words were wonderful and befitting a true, kind gentleman. My son was at my side, and he shed tears of his own, and I was proud at how composed he was and how loving. There were no hymns, but wonderful wartime songs played out and carefully thought out prose was spoken and a tear-jerker of a reading from a step-cousin which brought a very personal and real touch to the service.

I can't explain why I felt so empty, I think it might have been because my dad lost his dad, and he finally let out tears, tears I suspect he had been holding back. It took a giant, genuine hug from three daughters, Diary, to set them free and wash out his pain. I was soaked — from sweaty excretions, not tears — from the minute I sat down to the minute I got home later. I was hoping to keep my coat on which presented me in some sort of curvaceous shape, but I was so hot, I had to undo it and waft my grandad's service leaflet about my face. The HRT hadn't kicked in, so I had to just go with it. I watched my handsome grandad in

Carla Day

his bow-tie pass my face over and over as the sweat grew in ferocity and the need to fan it away overtook the need to be polite. I was so glad to be outside after the service and in the cool air I almost yelped with relief.

I didn't wear the dress, Diary, because on the second fitting I looked more than ridiculous and have no idea what I was thinking. When you are fat, avoid dresses, full stop. I sat in one spot at the wake and didn't circle the room. I left that to Middle

Sister, the social butterfly. I was just waiting for it to be over, so I could get to my little sister's house and eat pizza and catch up with news and watch my nephews, just watch them and drink them in because I crave them when I'm away. My brother-inlaw orders the most spectacular pizza topping combination, and I only ever eat it there. I was very much looking forward to the next day too. I would finally get to see my mum and look into her eyes because she will be relieved I'm finally there in the room. I know I'll feel a bit shitty I left it so long.

Dear Diary,

Home at Last

Christmas Eve arrived, and I was tucked away at my middle sister's house with my family around me, and my brother-in-law didn't even mention my digs at him in my forthcoming book — I admired his composure and even realised I'd forgiven him a long time ago and even began to like him as I did when we initially met. My sister had also put on weight, Diary, and it didn't matter anyway. None of the weight battles I'd cried over mattered. All that mattered was in that room smiling familiar smiles and sitting around a glistening twelve-foot tree. Kids were running around and the French bulldog jumping all over the place and life felt as it should, normal. After the magical visit to my mum's, life began to feel okay again. Sitting in Mum's room the day before, I was glad it was just the two of us for a few hours. I saw her eyes light up the room with magic, Diary, and she sighed with relief because her eldest daughter was finally there in the room. I took in a spicy-smelling Christmas candle and ornaments and decorations and photos and we talked. I had saved a lot to tell her, and it was lovely to watch her scan my face and take in all she could. I could tell how pleased she was. I repeated, perhaps too much, just how much I hated living so many miles away and how much I missed her, and as I sounded out the words, I suddenly felt torn between living a life for me and coming to be with her because time is running out for her, and I know when that time comes, I'll be a mess. The room was cosy, and Christmas-y and I really enjoyed every second of our time, playing silly games and talking for the sake of it because it was so nice to hear her gentle voice.

At Middle Sis's, we drank and chatted and lay the kids' presents under the tree in a haphazard fashion, and the whole evening was warm and natural. Christmas morning was spent watching the kids undo a huge amount of gifts and then we went for a walk along the canal while the boys prepped and cooked a feast fit for a king. Marvellous indeed, Diary, and I only had a few manageable sweats as the HRT began to do its dirty work. My

One Leg Out

poor boy had one of his intense migraines on Christmas day and missed out on dinner but was with us during the evening, looking peaky, but joining in the fun. I worry about the frequency of them. On my way back home in the car after a short few days, I was glad to be going home. Dad was very brave, but I noticed a few wobbly moments as the emotional day unfolded. I wondered what he was thinking. He doesn't elaborate on his feelings, but I know when he's sad inside. I managed to temporarily put the menopause to one side and focus on what really mattered, although I have felt a bit snappy with my partner. I hope my madness is not coming back again.

Dear Diary,

What A Worry

When I was putting the world to rights with Lil' Sister on the day of Grandad's funeral, I received a text from the husband of a friend I had become quite close to during a two-year period in a remote location. It wasn't good news, not at all. 'The big C had wormed its way into their family.' I managed to contain my sadness until I got home and went to the hospital to visit and try my best to comfort my friend in what was a totally shitty situation. She was brave, and we talked as we always had, rushing to share news but the undertone of panic she concealed with smiles didn't fool me. I hate illness and especially when it touches those I love and care about. She's doing well, the op went well, I'm praying that's it for her, Diary, and our chats continue for a very long time.

Update, Diary, it hasn't spread, and she's going to be okay. Ah, I can breathe again now.

Carla Day

Dear Diary,

Something's Gotta Give

There was something deeply poignant about yesterday's dog walk, it wasn't as pleasurable as other times. I had a strange sense that, although I'm free of menopausal symptoms — at least physical ones — there is little change to my mind and the intermittent depression that lurks.

I think, Diary, if I'm honest, I'm generally unhappy on the inside. I don't know if the reason is the primarily HRT and the mild anxiety it brings, or if I need to change the way I live my life. I've concluded my life isn't very exciting. In fact, I can say it's quite boring. I don't seem to do half the stuff I used to and that, Diary, is down to me because I've settled for couple-dom and domestic life and I've completely forgotten how to be carefree. I had a moment of pure panic, the way you do when you've lost something precious.

The bitterly cold day made me shiver and exhale out, long smoky wisps. I sauntered along, impossibly unentertained by nature. Even the myriad waterfowl, and fluffy clouds, and grass on the banks, which had curled from the ice cold and were white and crisp, didn't excite. They are things that usually bring a smile to my face, ordinary pockets of nature, snatches of wonder, sights to behold, but not that day

The scenery felt all-too-familiar and I'm an adventurer, I love to see and experience new things, and I'm not doing any of it at present. It was nice, however, to feel the cold slipping down my collar and seep into my bones, because I had been hot and sweaty for so long it was an actual pleasure to have my teeth chattering. I must have looked a bit deranged smiling my way through the shudders of cold.

As I walked my usual route, I began to crave new sights, a surprise around the corner. I know the walk so well I could close my eyes and imagine it and stay at home save myself the bother. Of course, that's not why I go, Diary. It's to please the senses and the clearing of one's mind. I guess I feel as though I've stopped being the adventurer. I need to change this and start to motivate

Carla Day

myself into being me again.

I used to walk miles and miles, around untrodden corners with no fear, only anticipation. I would happily go anywhere. Lately, and I'm not sure if the menopause is to blame, but I've stopped, and my walks have become inane and normal dog walking plods, down lanes and across the same old beaches — which I'm incredibly lucky to have on doorstep — but I need bigger panoramic views and stunning vistas farther away.

My partner, due to dodgy knees, has stopped walking for the time being, and I miss our walks massively. It was part of our binding-together, those beautiful outdoors experiences. Maybe I should join a rambling club or pack my rucksack and just go, roll on, spring. Nothing new has enthused me for far, far too long and that simply must change.

New Year's resolution: Find myself in new places, seeking new things.

Dear Diary,

Sort Your Shit Out

I really need to get a grip, today as my son drove off on his first driving lesson, I had a lump in my throat and tears in my eyes. I'm not sure it's just me. Do other people seem to cry at literally anything, or am I'm completely alone in my sensitivity? I'm super proud of him, Diary, as you know, but it's getting beyond ridiculous. Anyhow, I'm feeling more positive today. My feeling of this year being the year of change is even more prevalent in my thoughts. I can't wait to get started.

Carla Day

It would be amazing if a smidgen of sunlight would show up to help with my mood. But if it doesn't, I'm not made of sugar, and a little rain won't dissolve me. I intend to do this properly: gym, walks, diet, and even a bit of meditation to get me through those dark doubting moments. Now, Diary, as you know, I've been here before but believe it was at the wrong time of year — not that there ever is a right one to get fit — but now coming into spring, the mind is fuller of spirit and just to hear the birds singing in tree tops gives you a boost. So, I am going to leap into this year with gusto and, Diary, if I show up here again ranting about how sad I feel, kick my backside, will you?

My diet alone could help me shed the parts of me I detest. If I stop grazing like a cow, maybe, just maybe, I have a fighting chance. I might even have a go at being Diary and gluten free. It's worked for friends who are looking decidedly lean and have glowing skin, so it could work. The HRT is kicking in, I am able to get some sleep, and my sheets are dry. That may sound like a small thing, but when you are genuinely almost suicidal from lack of sleep and being permanently soaked, its huge news.

My forgetfulness, however, remains, and I did something I'm ashamed of. I left my phone charger at work. What's so shameful about that, you might ask? Well, I didn't remember leaving it at work and accused my other half's kids who were with us for the weekend of stealing it. I was convinced that they had taken it and wouldn't admit to me the truth, and Diary, I got the right hump and threw the biggest hissy fit. It was only when I returned to

One Leg Out

work I found it right there on the counter that I cringed at my stomping around the house like a mental person, shouting: 'I know one of you's had it, bastards!' Mmm, the less said about that the better, and I still haven't managed to tell them yet.

Dear Diary,

Skating on Thin Ice

While watching Michael Portilo's, *Great British Railway Journeys*, a particular memory came to mind, and I needed to document it before it disappeared. A long, long time ago when I was seeing a man from Greece, and he was over visiting, we had gone to Portsmouth, and from there went on the hovercraft to the adjacent island: The Isle of White. It turned into a very funny outing and reminded me of how close I once was with said sister. We decided to go to an ice rink as the island seemed deserted and there wasn't much else to do. The Greek was, for want of a better phrase, a bit cocky.

One Leg Out

He was overly confident in most areas of life and that day was no different. Fortunately for him, the rink was also empty, and we put on our skates and set off on the ice, a little shaky but enjoying the fun. Me and my middle sis shot off, having a go and not noticing the Greek-ex clinging on to the side with both hands while his feet went another way altogether.

We stopped to watch as he made his debut across the ice, not actually moving his feet but wheeling his arms to make him go. We saw way before he did how this was going to end and predicted his fall from grace as he grinned with uneasy confidence. He face-planted the floor shortly after, and we heard his nose crack.

We were the other side of the rink, Diary, and couldn't get to him for two reasons. One, we were laughing too much and two, we couldn't skate very well. I saw blood spreading across the ice, but the Greek still claimed he was fine and still grinned with blood in his teeth, and we laughed until we cried. That might sound cruel, Diary, but you didn't know him, and I guess you had to be there. It was an amusing day and the laughter about it continued long after and still makes me chuckle. May he rest in peace.

Carla Day

Dear Diary,

On It Like a Car Bonnet

Mission accomplished, I've brought a week's worth of very healthy foods and drinks, and I'm all set to go. Yes, I know, you've heard it all before. I felt very proud of my shopping trolley and saw a few approving glances at my very colourful, overflowing-with-goodness mound. I pushed that cart around the supermarket, throwing in everything green with my head held high, and I was raring to go. Then, I reached the checkout and almost had a heart attack. The bill for this healthy eating malarkey — which I should have remembered from the other times — was extortionate.

One Leg Out

Diary, I didn't care. After my initial bum-twitching moment, I decided I would be very happy to spend all my wages on getting fit. Yes, Diary, and as if by magic or some kind of karmic fate, my lil' sister emailed me a photo she dug out of me and Middle Sis looking super skinny and happy doing the three-legged-race at my son's nursery. If that isn't a big fat incentive, then I don't know what is.

The sun is shining as if by magic, and my state-of-mind is positive. Now, Diary, that could just be me having a sort-of bipolar episode. I've never been diagnosed, but I do have these euphoric moments or days followed by a slump in mood and a depressed time. Hopefully, I'm just happy to be kicking my own butt, let's see. I pray for sunshine, momentum, consistency, and willpower to get me through these next weeks. I'm determined this time.

Dear Diary,

Merry-Go-Round

I woke this morning feeling hormonal. I opened my eyes to my white bedroom ceiling, trying to focus through the network of veiny floaters, reminding me I need to check out my eyesight with a new optometrist that doesn't insist on eating curry right before my eye exam. Diary, you know it's going to be a tough day when you are tearful before your brain has had a chance to engage in thought of any kind. On reflection, the day before I might have taken an extra HRT pill. I couldn't remember if I'd taken one, so I took another just in case. Still clueless.

I wouldn't mind but there in a packet with the days written on, and I still take them randomly, such is my brain. So, I may have overdosed a little on estrogen. That could be the answer to the morning's foggy head and floods of tears over my morning cuppa which didn't taste right. Sometimes, Diary, I truly hate being a woman. I don't like the unpredictability of my moods, only yesterday I wanted to kiss the clouds and dance on them and be this new ball of energy.

Today my spiraling temper and inner rage, I'm sure, must be pushing my blood pressure up. Why, I'm not entirely sure, never am, it's all guess-work, one big fucking menopausal puzzle.

Anyhow, I forced myself up and out of the house, ditching the cycle I had planned with my deflated-looking partner. I needed to be alone and to clear my head because I felt my snappiness surging, and I wouldn't want to be around me, Diary. I made a promise to myself that I was going to do energetic things on my days off, so, I swung my legs out of bed, got dressed, paying little effort to my image and shot off in the car with my trusty doggy companion and my hair a bit Worzel Gummidge-like.

The first part of the walk, Diary, I was a mess. The reservoir is a calm place I have been before but not for a while. I'm on my search of new places, as you know, but that was just the right remedy for brain farts. I also decided that when I'm off on a new venture, I must reward myself after, so when it becomes grueling, there is something to look forward to, and the café at the reservoir serves real coffee — fresh, aromatic, ground, and rich — and I could scribble my notes there too. That was my reward along with some pretty enigmatic views.

As I said, my eyes were heavy, loaded with tears for the first ten minutes. The sky was heavy too, creating a gun-metal grey, moody atmosphere. It threatened rain and my dog followed me quietly, looking forlorn and a bit worried because she's a sensitive dog and picks up on my mood, I plodded on feeling very sorry for myself.

Out of nowhere, a robin appeared, right in front of me on a post and, Diary, the sight of it made me sob. Now, I know it might sound daft, but I saw a post once on social media that said if you see a robin while out walking, the spirit of a loved one that has passed away is trying to get in touch. In light of my grandad's recent passing, and others I loved dearly, I clearly saw this as I sign.

It could be me, but that tiny robin hopped and flittered from post to post, all the way along the path, always in front of me, until we reached the open space by the top reservoir, then it vanished. The sun came out at the precise moment the robin showed up and was strong and bright for the rest of the walk.

How bizarre. I felt like that little morsel of a bird with its rouged chest was encouraging me to walk through the tears and the frustration and to keep going until my head was free of thinking and, by golly, worked.

By the time I reached the bridge on the reservoir, my mood was as light as can be, and I scanned the surrounding sunbathed hills and tall spiky forest, and deep blue water and breathed in those beautiful countryside smells. I stood and watched sheep grazing on the hillside and a couple of red kites circling, and the day suddenly seemed glorious. I was able to laugh at my earlier mood and even enjoyed a slow walk back along the path where a small stream trickled. The sound of it was so soothing, I slowed my pace some more, so I didn't miss anything interesting.

All I can say, Diary, is thank God for the countryside and Welsh views, they do help my sanity and help me get perspective on stuff.

One thing that did concern me and throw me off a bit was a sight on the return walk. I was thinking about my relationship and how difficult this must be for my partner, when I came across a pair of gloves on the path, right in front of me. Now, Diary, I'm not religious, as you know, but I am quite superstitious. If I see a black cat coming toward the path I'm on, Diary, I run like the clappers. I was told a long time ago, after purchasing a pair of gloves for a boyfriend, that they are a parting gift. I was dumped shortly after handing them over and it's stuck with me ever since. Is my relationship doomed? I don't have time to think about additional worries, let's hope he can put up with me until I figure this menopause thing out.

The coffee was so superb, I drank two cups and it was quiet and I wrote and jotted down notes and people-watched which is a much-revered pastime.

I don't ever feel lonely on these walks and jaunts of mine. I love how much there is to see. Life is rich in the simplest of forms. I watched a mother enjoying a minute of tranquility while her newborn suckled. She looked at her child, not moving her gaze once, while sipping on a cup of tea, I could see how much she was enjoying and capsulating the moment. An old man sat with his middle-aged daughter, they were chatting, his eyes smiling, and a man in a wheelchair, who must have had a degenerative disease, as he couldn't move a jot, not even his head, only his mouth. But he was enjoying a cuppa too, with the aid of a very caring, devoted wife. It was nice to see these things. I like how you can tell by someone's eyes what they are saying. Well, today's walk sorted out my muddled thinking, my irritable mood and a whole jumble of other gripes and unnoteworthy cod's wallop.

I felt as fresh as a daisy afterwards, God bless the great outdoors. Yes, I'm an atheist but it's something we say, anyway, isn't it? Maybe I should make something else up that's less hypocritical. How about, "Thank the stars for our glorious countryside."

That's better, eh, Diary?

One Leg Out

Dear Diary,

Fresh as a Daisy

On my quest to visit new places for my walks, I found another gem. I'd been before briefly and had wanted to revisit to explore the forest and reservoir. I can feel a surge in my energy levels, and I'm chomping at the bit to get out and about, especially if there is sunshine to be had.

Today, Diary, the walk went far beyond my expectations of a good walk. For some reason, there was clarity to my mind, a real sharpness. My thoughts were clear and fog free and I felt on top

Carla Day

of the world. It was a wonderful feeling. The sun was celestial-bright and cast a glossy, golden sheen over everything: the water, the grass, the trees, frost on the path, and even the hills in the distance. The colours were so intense, mostly sumptuous golds and vivid greens and blues, the pictures they painted were stunning, mesmerizing. I watched the dramatic scenery from a bench and found it difficult to get up and leave because it was almost too pretty.

The day was magical and because it was Monday, I practically had the whole place to myself. It was nice to not think, Diary, but to just enjoy every sight, every view from the glistening movement of the water to the swaying tree-tops and all in between. It was so wonderful I had to walk around it twice to take everything in. Maybe the HRT is kicking in after all and doing its job, or maybe it was just a bloody good day. I felt alive and the crispness of the air as I breathed it down I felt reaching deep into my lungs. Any stress that might have been present was siphoned right out of me, Diary. I took so many photos the memory on my phone ran out. And, as for "icing on the cake," Costa coffee only went and introduced coconut coffee to their menu, and it was absolutely delicious. My little friend smiled all the way around, did you know that, Diary, dogs actually smile when they're happy, I love that.

I have training with work again tomorrow, I really don't like it.

I want to go off walking instead, oh well.

Dear Diary

New Office

After another lovely walk and plenty of sunshine, I felt full of energy and decided to release that energy on the spare room that has long needed an overhaul. I rummaged through our shed which was a feat in itself and found the wallpaper stripper and within three hours it was stripped of the old dowdy wallpaper and the walls looked like a blank canvass where I could unleash my creativity. I was so chuffed with myself for getting on with something. I spent an hour planning the colour scheme and drawing out how I wanted it to look on paper. I found everything, wallpaper, paint shades, and quilt sets. I imagined it done and was excited. I'm desperate for an office space, and this would double up just nicely. Before my partner got home, I had cleaned up and expected that he would be fully supportive and as excited as me to finally be moving forward with decorating a room.

My enthusiasm was immediately dashed as his first look was one of someone who isn't impressed at all.

'What's up?' No reply, scans the area and can't find anything wrong because I did a thorough job, but I know he's looking for something to complain about. I know he's a practical man, but a 'Well done, baby,' would have been nice.

'We'll have to get this skimmed before you paint.' Scratches his beard and at this point I want to poke him in the eye because it's not bad enough to warrant money for a plasterer, and I know he's being a pedantic knob.

'But it's a good job. The plaster's not bad at all, a bit of rubbing down and filler where the small holes are from old screws and it will be as good as new.'

'No, it needs skimming, and the skirting boards need to come off, they're too small.' I knew instantly that even though I'd done a good job, he needed to be in control and take over a project. I was so deflated and stuffed my drawings away, because he was so negative about it all. I just wanted to be away from him. What is it about men relinquishing control to a woman when it comes to decorating? I should have waited until he was away and just got on with it. Then any minor changes needed would be just that. Men can be dicks. Anyway, just a minor gripe, Diary. I know I could do an amazing job and, on a budget too, and I will.

I know he's a perfectionist, but the problem with that is he doesn't have the funds to be one, so sometimes a budget job done lovingly and carefully can be just as good, and you don't have to wait forever to live in a clean, fresh-looking house. This project I want to be just mine, so I can show him just how brilliant I can be. I can be stubborn too, and I'm not giving up MY project.

Update: Diary, a week later and the skirting boards are staying, and we are not having a plasterer as the walls are deemed ok with a good rub down. Wink, wink.

Dear Diary,

I Have a Bit of a Confession

While out walking in dense woodlands in the middle of nowhere, I desperately needed to pee. This annoying desire to wee-on-demand I attribute to the menopause. As soon as I drink anything, not just caffeine, I have to go within the hour, sometimes, immediately. It's a sudden burning urge and when this happens, I usually find a large rock or tree trunk to duck behind when there are no toilets in the vicinity, obviously.

Now, Diary, I'm pretty experienced at peeing outdoors. It's not something I'm proud of but as long as you are discreet and use biodegradable tissue, I don't see the problem. I usually take time

One Leg Out

to scan the area while waddling cross-legged to find a suitable spot to squat, and if the coast is clear, it's all systems go, and the relief is usually second to none.

On this occasion the spot was a dip behind a tree with enough tall grass in front of me to not expose my foof should the unavoidable happen which it never does. Somehow, Diary, I failed to spot a pair of well-to-do dog walkers in waxy jackets and Hunter wellies. They must have appeared around the corner the very minute I'd looked away.

I dropped behind the tree and relieved myself, then, stood to retrieve a tissue from my pocket, only to be greeted by a large, curious silver Weimaraner and a very unamused posh-looking couple. They politely looked away and walked on shouting, 'Come, Monty, leave the lady alone.' I dropped down and did the quickest wipe ever. I didn't get back up until they were out of sight. The humiliation was instant, even though I was quite within my rights to have a wee.

I didn't feel very ladylike, Diary, and heat rose in my face until I glowed like my dad's barbecue in the summer of 2012. They must have been ninja dog walkers as I didn't even hear their footsteps. I hope they had a good laugh at it, Diary, and didn't go home to tell all their neighbours that they saw a bag-lady pissing in the woods.

I hadn't even brushed my hair that day, and I was covered in mud splats as I'd been hiking off-the-beaten-track with my trusty dog and had slipped into a muddy puddle. In my defense, I was in dog walking mode, not catwalk and had on old, tatty clothes. Oh, my God, they probably thought I was a dirty, homeless person. I can't be the only person to pee when out in the countryside, surely?

I consider myself to be a respectable woman, liberal-minded and fortunately able to laugh at myself. The thought of someone thinking I'm a nut-job who defecates in the woods for the sake of it is just shameful and maybe a little comic. On the plus side, Diary, when you are in a field, on top of a hill, where you have a three-hundred-and-sixty-degree view and know for certain you aren't going to get caught, there's nothing like an outdoor pee with wind around your foof and the sun on your face.

Or is that just me? Ha.

Dear Diary,

Brrr

I think it's fair to say I don't care much for winter. I think I suffer from Seasonal Adjustment Disorder, just to make my list of crap-to-deal-with even larger. I do feel depressed, more so on dark gloomy days, especially when it's raining, and I want to go out exploring and can't because there is so much mud, I might as well go mud wrestling instead and, Diary, well, just no. I think that a regular dose of vitamin D can keep those nasties at bay.

I've recently looked into a range of different ways to combat the menopause: phytoestrogens, bioidentical estrogens, going on a plant-based diet. None of which, for me at least, are a realistic path. Not because I wouldn't try new things, Diary, as I've considered everything but because the HRT I'm currently taking is keeping everything at bay apart from a little moodiness, but I have that either on or off so, I'm going to try and deal with them best I can when they show up and hope I don't bite my tongue off while trying to stay calm. Let's see. I'm sticking to healthy diet and exercise as and when I can. I'm still doing the stairs pajama run when I'm alone and can't be arsed to get dressed, and I've recently discovered YouTube exercise videos for those days when I do not want to leave the house and, Diary, I love them. I can choose the part of me I want to tighten and go for it and even pause when I'm knackered. I'm okay in the love department too, lube is still an essential item of the bedroom but in general, lovemaking happens more often, and I'm not sighing anymore when my partner hints at sex.

I'm still waiting for spring to break and for the warm days to arrive, so I can stay outdoors for longer and keep up with the new places to visit. I've found some great vintage markets to go to soon and other things of interest to do outdoors that are local. When it rains, and I'm stuck inside, I close my eyes and imagine what it will be like in the summer when I can sit on a beach and stare at the sea and read a stack of books and get that tan going. I'm lucky that I'm next to the sea and can do these wonderful things. Today is one of those dreary days, Diary, and my car battery has died, and I've just signed up for a course that is going to take up a lot of my spare time. It's not a course that interests me, but I will need it should I wish to climb the ladder at work. Oh, well, it's for free so I shouldn't grumble.

Lately, I've been thinking a lot about when I was a kid and how I was pretty bad at catching a ball and how I would more so have it hit my face than actually catch it - my Dad delighted in reminding me of this. I used to have very little hand-eye coordination and bad coordination in general, especially at dance and exercise classes. I would be the one at the back who would be stepping right instead of left and moving my arm out to slap someone's face as they stepped toward me. In salsa classes, I would take the role of the man because I found it impossible to take direction on being the girl, subsequently leading to me getting thrown out and my dance partner refusing to dance with me. The one sport I excelled at was running but then it was difficult to mess up putting one foot in front of the other. I was chosen to run for the county, representing my primary school. The problem was I didn't listen properly to the track instructor and fear had gripped me with sizable force. I completely froze when the gun sounded off. It was a slow-motion delayed reaction, and I came last because by the time I figured out how to get my foot out of the trap and try and catch up my competitors, it was all over, and the taunts didn't go away for years. I swear the P.E. teacher eyeballed me for coming in last and making a tit out of him and our school. It felt great some

Carla Day

years later when my son was on the same track representing the same school and won every race. That, Diary, was truly awesome.

I suppose the reason for these thoughts were brought on by the pre-test for the course I just signed up for. I had to do English and Math. I aced the English, but the Math result was rubbish, so I had to re-sit it. Thankfully, I passed the second time, but the stress of it took me back to being a child with little self-confidence and all I could think about were the things I was crap at, and I almost had a panic attack, how daft, eh, Diary?

The boy has taken to sitting in his room, studying but is reluctant to get a part-time job. He is employing diversion tactics, but I'm not fooled. If he doesn't have a job in two weeks' time or at very least a few interviews lined up, he will find himself with no Xbox, or laptop. Let's see how quickly he moves then, Diary. I'm sick of asking nicely.

Dear Diary.

Vikings and Stupidness

I have to report to you a minor observation that made me chuckle.

I've come to realise that my flippant remarks don't serve me well, and I must try and curb them. The other day, purely as an observation you'll understand, I happened to mention that my partner looked a bit Viking-ish.

He answered: 'Because I have a beard?'

'Yes, and because you're blond and have that look,' I answered, thinking that was the end of my compliment.

'What's that look, then?' I have to think carefully now because

Carla Day

I know I could offend.

'You know, sort of Nordic.' My smile was sweet.

'You mean I look scruffy?' he asks, scratching his beard. 'No, I mean unkempt, but in a kind of cute, rugged way.' 'Kind of?' He says.

FFS, I think to myself but answer: 'Yes, kind of.'

He took it the wrong way, Diary, you can't even pay people a compliment these days.

'Should I shave my beard off?' came next, and I couldn't help but sigh and do an eye-roll.

'No.'

I must have answered a tad too quickly because his reply came at me quicker than a tennis ball.

'Do I look jowly without a beard?' Now, Diary, I thought *I* was self-conscious.

'Now you're being stupid.' I said, hoping he doesn't contemplate losing his whiskers which I have grown very fond of.

Another regrettable statement I made lately was to my son, who I considered was being lazy, sat in bed watching TV. In reality, he was in his room relaxing after a week at college, you know, chilling.

I was in cleaning mode, so his chilling annoyed me, and I had to open his door and say this:

'You are getting lazy, you need to move your arse and get a job. No son of mine is going to sit on his backside watching telly all day. You need to be responsible and show willing or you'll end

One Leg Out

up working at McDonald's.'

Not that there's anything wrong with it, in fact I hear they're a good employer, but I want so much more for him. I know he's dealing with his A levels and that brings its own stress.

Seriously though, he does need a part-time job.

He looked at me in despair, shook his head and said, 'Please shut the door.'

Diary, I did, I shut the door and thought, *What the hell am I doing?* I got so fired up at his nonchalant attitude, I burst through the door and made him jump.

'You live under my roof, eat my food, and use my car as a taxi and as your mum, I do it out of love but as my son, I expect respect and contribution because you're a decent human being, got it?' My voice was amplified and slightly demonic. I must have pissed off my neighbours.

'Okay, Mum, I'll start looking.' He looked a little terrified, but I felt sort of better getting it off my chest, and I even managed to do it without swearing.

So, okay, Diary, tact isn't my thing lately. Maybe I should have approached it differently and sat on his bed to explain why I'm frustrated with him? I should have reasoned because ranting helps no one, especially me. I went downstairs, abandoned the cleaning and was tearful because it felt wrong even though in principle I was right.

I thought about this for a bit and knew if someone had walked into my room shouted at me while I was enjoying a relaxing hour

Carla Day

or two, I would have flipped. Am I the only frustrated parent out there?

I doubt it, Diary.

Dear Diary,

Life

Thinking back to when I first met my partner, it was a fairytale time, but as life's tragic events grew in ferocity, that fairytale became fractured. Not because of anything relationship related but because life can take it out on you and taint everything good when bad stuff happens you can't control.

It's funny how one side of your life seems perfect while the mirror reflection of the other side is struck with grief, sadness, worry, chaos, and is generally dark. The brain really can handle some dark, complicated shit. Seeing as my relationship survived my mini-breakdown, I can only assume that is stronger because

Carla Day

of it and that any niggles we do have are purely stupid everyday ones and possibly down to my menopause and his stubbornness.

I think I keep looking backward because I'm unsure of what the future looks like. I know there are things I would like to fix. Superficial things, like being thinner, fitter, I know younger isn't an option but being generally healthier is. I also think that reaching middle age means you assess everything about your life and where you are at. Most importantly, you ask yourself if you are happy and menopause aside, I think I am.

I reflect a lot because I do compare my memories and experiences with those I'm currently having and perhaps I shouldn't. I keep them handy for a kind of reference exercise. To see if they're as good or even better, when in reality they are so different, comparing is just silly. I'm going off on a tangent, Diary. This constant reflection could be because there are so many important changes when the menopause happens and the sudden jolt into middle age makes you grasp at what little tendrils of youth are still apparent — I can confirm there are very few.

You know, Diary, I hadn't even considered in all my agonizing about the time-of-life, that I can no longer produce children, not that I ever wanted more but still, it's weird and a bit sad. That's the least of my worries. That thought does make you look to the future more tentatively though, Diary, because you can't hide from age. The middle age thing is a scary section of life when you come across death, loss, disease, and other frightening stuff that makes you think hard about your own mortality.

When you reach middle age, a lot of people give up the fight because it's easy to do just that. They wear baggy clothes, stop wearing make-up, eat mountains of unhealthy food, bingewatch mindless TV, and grind to an agonizing halt which only equals boredom and death. I saw this happen with some of my mum's very glamorous friends who I'd considered pathetic for giving up and looking raggedy and old. Of course, I was a teenager at the time and knew nothing about the menopause. Young people can be idiots, eh, Diary?

As for my future, I want to live it smiling, enjoying, and keeping busy. I do too much thinking and not enough living. It's time to start thinking less and living more.

As for the menopause, I'm learning — sometimes through gritted teeth — to live with it and manage it. Whenever I need to pay it attention and change things, I will, because it's an ever-changing beast that can dictate my physical and emotional being. I have to deal with it in segments and alter my menopause plan accordingly.

I also remind myself that while I'm happily slating that beast for all of my untimely misfortune, some woman will never get to experience getting older and the menopause because they were terribly unlucky. So, I must be grateful just for being alive, and being able to immerse myself in small pleasures that are unique to me, and I suppose, for the damned menopause.

So, dearest Diary, I'm going to sign off for a while at least and put those well intended plans into action. I need to start living. You've become a sterling listener, Diary, and a bit of an addiction, so I might be back one day, but for now, adios, amigo and thank you, SO MUCH!

***

One Leg Out

Carla Day

Glossary of UK terms

"The United States and Great Britain are two countries separated by a common language." - *George Bernard Shaw*.

Some UK slang might be unfamiliar to readers from other countries, this helpful glossary will soon have you talking and swearing like a citizen of the UK.

A levels - qualification pre-university

Adverts - advertisements

At it like knives - very sexually active

Bird - word for female

Biscuits - cookies

Bits - small pieces of information or a collection of small things

Bloody - equivalent of damn

Blowing out of my arse - it's tiring from physical exhaustion

Bombay mix - Indian spicy snack

Bugger - a local term of endearment meaning person

Bum - arse, backside, or bottom

Can't be arsed - can't be bothered

Car bonnet - car hood

Chinese whispers - like the telephone game in the US

Chuffed - very proud

Chuffing - fucked and fucking

Carla Day

Cocking - blooming or bloody. slang term

Cod's wallop - rubbish or nonsense

Cuppa - cup of tea

Doo-lally - crazy

Down the phone - on the telephone line

Eighteen skinny fits and not so skinny fits - jeans style and size

Faff - to mess around

Fancy - to imagine, ex: Fancy that! Or to like someone, ex: I fancy him.

Fit - hot, good looking

Fizzy drinks - soda

Floaters - small black spots in vision

Foof - slang for vagina, mostly in Wales

Fortnight - a period of two weeks

Fringe - bangs

Gits - idiots

Grumpy old sod - miserable person

Have the hump - being in a bad mood

Having a go - trying

Hokey cokey - an old Irish song that sings about putting a leg in and out of a circle, called Hokey pokey in the USA

HRT - hormone replacement therapy

Hunter wellies - make of Wellington rain boots

I was made up - happy

Jump leads - leads to start the car, from one engine to another

Kaky - poop or crap

Kip - sleep

Kitchen roll - paper towels

Knackered - tired

Knickers - ladies underwear, panties

Knob - dick or penis

Lie in - sleep in

Loo - toilet

Loo roll - toilet roll

Losing the plot - going crazy

Lot - family

M&S - Marks & Spencer, a popular store everywhere in the UK

Mac's - McDonald's

Mates - friends

Miss Trenchbull - stern female teacher from the movie Matilda

Moo - cow an UK expression for a female, as in silly cow

Nappy - diaper

Not long qualified - recently qualified

Nutter - crazy person

On one - in a particular mood, usually angry

Peaky - pale, sickly looking

Pessaries - medication in the form of a pill inserted into the rectum

Ping-pong bat - ping-pong paddle

Pink marigolds - dishwashing gloves

Posh champers lunch - champagne dinner

Carla Day

Prawn - shrimp

Pudding - stodgy dessert

Really pants present - horrible or rubbish

Red kites - type of large bird of prey, resident in Wales

QCF - Relevant qualifications in health and social care
(Qualifications and Credit Framework) Level 3

Roll on, spring - looking forward to spring

Shite - shit or crap

Shopping trolley - shopping cart

Show willing - show enthusiasm

Slating - berating

Smash - succeed

Snaffle - eat quickly

Sod's law - unlucky

Spot on - precisely

Stick two fingers up - reverse victory sign, rude gesture

Stone - imperial unit of mass, fourteen pounds

Taff - A Welsh person

Take away - fast food to go

Tea - drink or late afternoon meal

Telly - T.V.

The clappers - old saying meaning to run quickly

Till - cash register drawer

Tittle-tattle - pettiness

Train him up - educate him

Wee - small (Scottish) or urination UK wide

One Leg Out

Wind me up - annoy

Wonky - not straight

Worzel Gummidge - scarecrow character on British TV

Yeay - yes

Carla Day

About the Author

Carla was born in Leicestershire, England and currently resides in South Wales, UK with her understanding partner, genius son and naughty Jack Russell - Lilly.

She can be found on mountain tops, contemplating life, or sitting on a weather-beaten log at the beach, scribbling a novel.

Carla studied creative writing, screenplays, and writing for the radio with "The Writers Bureau" in 2012. She has been penning stories ever since.

One Leg Out is her second published novel. Carla writes a satirical and soulful, weekly column - Carla's Corner, for the website: Mistress of The Menopause, an online support group for women going through *The Change*.

Carla is menopausal.

Carla Day

38622764R00121

Printed in Great Britain
by Amazon